WHY
JESUS?

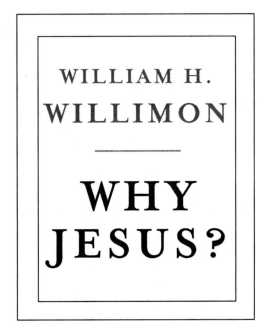

WILLIAM H.
WILLIMON

WHY
JESUS?

Abingdon Press
Nashville

WHY JESUS?

This book is printed on acid-free paper.

Library of Congress Cataloging-in-Publication Data

Willimon, William H.
   Why Jesus? / William H. Willimon.
      p. cm.
   ISBN 978-1-4267-0028-6 (trade pbk. : alk. paper)
   1. Jesus Christ—Person and offices. I. Title.
   BT203.W53 2010
   232'.8—dc22

2010029680

10 11 12 13 14 15 16 17 18 19—10 9 8 7 6 5 4 3 2 1

MANUFACTURED IN THE UNITED STATES OF AMERICA

To my students in the "Jesus Class" at Birmingham Southern College

CONTENTS

Introduction ix

1. Vagabond 1

2. Peacemaker 13

3. Storyteller 25

4. Party Person 37

5. Preacher 45

6. Magician 57

7. Home Wrecker 69

8. Savior 77

9. Sovereign 87

10. Lover 101

11. Delegator 113

12. Body 123

INTRODUCTION

Why Jesus? Because he is the most fascinating person in the world. Into my life he came, unsought and uninvited, took over, and refused to go. He led me into dangerous territory. Only later did I learn this is typical. Though he is one with us, he is neither casually nor promptly known, not because he is arcane but because he is so very different from us, so difficult to categorize or to define, because he is also one with God. You can know him for many years, yet never really know him as well as he appears to know you. He manages to be unfathomable, deep, ungraspable, and yet oddly close, intimate, talkative, and relentlessly relational.

Why Jesus? Why are billions of people sure that they know him as he really is and also confident that Jesus knows them as they are? Why have they not only adored him, sung songs to him, created grand works of art on account of him, erected great cathedrals in loving but futile attempt to enshrine him, but also have eagerly followed him, bet their lives upon him, and willingly gone where he leads them, even to die for him?

Why Jesus? I have some of the same challenges in describing Jesus as I have in describing Susan. Who is Susan, really?

Susan is a teacher. What would I tell you that might be most helpful in conveying who she is? Some Susan stories have become inflated over the years. After all, many agree that she is "quite a character." Susan has a history. Her family knows Susan in a way that I don't. Whether they know her better than I do is questionable, however. Sometimes those who are close to a person have difficulty obtaining a panoramic view.

"Why is Susan someone I should know?" I might reply, "Only time will tell her true significance. Come back thirty years after Susan is gone, and we'll see what of Susan is still with us." Some people are best known only in the backward glance.

But, of course, the best way to know *about* Susan would be to get to know her *personally*, as in opening your door to discover her there, spending an evening in conversation with her, allowing yourself to encounter her face-to-face. And that's what Christians believe Jesus does: he shows up at your place, wanting to introduce himself.

Why Jesus? My first answer is to remind you and me that if I can't adequately explain my friend and contemporary Susan (as the analogy above shows), then even less successful will be my attempt to introduce you to a Jew from Nazareth—who just happens to be God. Sometimes, looking for Jesus is like staring at the sun.

Why Jesus? I will tell stories other people have told about Jesus, anecdotes lovingly reiterated by the people who first met him. I'll work mostly from the four Gospels (Matthew, Mark, Luke, and John), following their goal of not attempting to reproduce a history of Jesus but rather to give a testimony to Jesus. The veracity of the gospel writers' testimony to Jesus is in their lives radically transformed by Jesus. I have great confidence in the accuracy of the four Gospels (the word gospel means "good news"), those strange literary devices that were concocted from twenty to a hundred years after the crucifixion of Jesus. (Throughout this book, I'll be referring to stories about Jesus from the Bible. You can find the passages in which these stories appear in the "You Can Look It Up" section in the back of this book).

The Gospels, and indeed all of Scripture, were born in a culture in which people passed information along orally, were careful to repeat things often, told only what was important, and looked for help from eyewitnesses to verify accuracy. The writers of the gospels collected the stories about Jesus that had been circulated orally and wove them into careful and distinctive accounts of what he said and did—and why that matters. Generations of Christians have found these writings to truly reveal God in singular and life-changing ways. Besides, we're justified in giving particular weight to the testimony of those who paid for their friendship with Jesus by their blood.

But Jesus is more than his words remembered; he is interesting not only because of what he said but for who he is. I will therefore also talk about Jesus through the medium of his friends. Paul (whose writings are older than the gospels) never met Jesus until the risen Christ accosted him on the Damascus Road. Yet Paul may know as much about Jesus as those who walked next to him down the Jerusalem Road. Paul seems neither to know nor to care about most of the teachings of Jesus or details of his life before the cross and resurrection, yet Paul's wildly adventurous life after meeting

Jesus shows that Paul really knows Jesus. We are right to trust descriptions of Jesus given by those most disrupted by Jesus. Some people around Jesus looked at him and wanted to follow him, pattern their lives after his, and tell everybody about him. The majority of people who met Jesus apparently thought he was nuts and wanted him dead. Sometimes, the burning sun is best viewed by watching those upon whom it shines.

Unlike presumed reconstructionists of the "historical Jesus," I shall not attempt to pick through the layers of accumulated wisdom about Jesus and dig down to what some contemporary historian thinks "really happened." A dearly loved principle of historians is *probability*, but the gospels present Jesus as a wild, weird, and improbable character. Aside from just one dismissive reference by the disreputable Josephus, Jesus made no impact on ancient historians. Most of what we hanker to know about Jesus is beyond historians' reach. The yield from two centuries of historical search for the "real" Jesus has been disappointing. I find delicious irony in the fact that Jesus changed the entire course of history but was ignored by historians of his day. Historians tended not to care about Galilean peasants who neither wrote books nor led armies.

While my presentation of Jesus benefits from the work of historians, mere world history was never an adequate vehicle for Jesus. Jesus' life and death demand high drama, not historical documentary. The gospel writers were more poets, preachers, and novelists than historical biographers of Jesus. Not content to dig up mere history, the gospels tell just enough of the story of a Jew who forever changed history to make you want to follow him. That's fine with me. I've never been told life-changing truth except by poets, novelists, and preachers. You want to know, "Why Jesus?" Well, let me tell you some stories.

Some of these stories involve the church's present-day experience of Jesus. Millions believe that, by the grace of God, they know Jesus quite well enough to follow him, even to follow through suffering and death. I shall say about Jesus what is said about him in Scripture by his earliest friends and enemies and also what is said in the lives of his followers today and down through the ages.

When I was trying to describe Susan to you, it became clear that the most important things about her—who she really is, what her life is all about— aren't things you can verify empirically. The same is true, of course, with Jesus. But still, we must take care not to diverge from the verifiable details about Jesus: that he was Jewish, worked exclusively in Judea, lived in a country occupied by the Roman army, called disciples, told stories, had compassion for the suffering, was a notorious troublemaker who went to lots of parties, was tortured to death after a short run as a wandering rabbi. Finally, we know that a group of his once-disheartened followers believed that he came back from the dead. These are the "facts on the ground" that the gospels and the letters of Paul tell us about Jesus. Taken together, allowed to speak with their delightful peculiarities, these earliest witnesses to Jesus give us a trustworthy, irreplaceable rendition of him, the most interesting person in the world. We must meet Jesus as presented by his first followers, or we meet him not at all.

I'll admit that it's odd to place your trust in a set of two-thousand-year-old writings—unless those writings just happen to be the real truth about God and us.

It's clear when we read the gospels that we are not reading some myth that took place in an imaginary Disneyland. Picking them up, you can almost taste the dust of Galilee. The people who met Jesus are real people with real-life concerns. Knowledge of the historical and cultural context of Jesus protects us from the sin of making Jesus mean anything we want. People have fantasized Jesus to be a proto-liberationist revolutionary, the boyfriend of Mary Magdalene, a savvy corporate CEO, a roving psychotherapist, a spiritual guru—and that's just this year's books about him. Paul had some choice words for those who preach "another Jesus" than the one who meets us in the specifics of the tradition.[1] We don't know everything we might like to know about Jesus, but we know enough to keep us from projecting on him our ideas of a more congenial savior.

Few followers of Jesus trudge after him on the basis of historical details. It's who Jesus is and yet shall be that is most compelling. So in telling you about Jesus, I shall not exclude my own meager testimony. There is a sense in which the contemporary followers of Jesus—that bumbling, sometimes faithful, though often feckless body known as the church—know more about him than his first disciples. This is not simply because his first followers are routinely represented in the gospels as blithering fools. It's also because Simon Peter and the rest of the disciples were around Jesus for less time than we have been. The longer you know someone, the better you know him or her, particularly if he or she is determined to be known by you. Most of us don't discover Jesus; he discovers us.

One day, "some Greeks" came to Jesus' disciples saying, "We want to see Jesus."[2] Is that what you want too? Do you want to see the one who came from dry, dusty Galilee, moved under the cold gaze of peasants, a man destitute, without job, house, or welcoming family? Do you want to see this one who, though he had nothing, refused to act like a submissive, cringing simpleton but stood up to the presumed powerful and dared to speak directly for God, tackling sickness and death and taxes head on, facing down both demons and swaggering, sword-wielding bullies? Do you want to see this one who, though he appeared so ordinary, made such wild, reckless claims for himself, reaching out to the dead, the dying, and the demented? Do you want to see this one whom we dare to believe is God with us? If so, then the invitation of this book is simple: come and see.

Neither two thousand years of familiarity nor the frequent cluelessness of his present-day disciples have dampened the world's enthusiasm for Jesus. A higher number of the world's people now follow Jesus than ever before, and as many are murdered for joining Jesus' swelling chorus as in times of past persecution.

John's Gospel begins with emissaries sent out to the wilderness by the religious bigwigs in Jerusalem to interrogate a wild preacher known as John the Baptizer.[3] They ask John, "Who are you?" and also who is this "one coming after" whom you say is "mightier"? The Baptizer tells them, in effect, that they will have difficulty getting their heads around the real identity of the Christ. Jesus is someone who shatters our preconceptions of just how a Messiah is supposed to talk and to act. "Among you stands one whom you do not know, the one who is coming after me," says John, "the one whom I am unworthy to tie his shoelaces."

Jesus remains the "one whom you do not know," even for people like me who have spent a lifetime trying to know him better. If you are reading this book and feel that you don't know much about Jesus, that's a good thing. In my experience, it's the folks who think they really, really know Jesus who don't know him that well at all.

I want publicly to thank Jesus for saying "Follow me!" and thereby making my world more interesting than if he had not risked all on me. Be warned: in reading this book, you are taking a risk of getting discombobulated, commandeered, and befriended by the most interesting person in the world.

Will Willimon

YOU CAN LOOK IT UP

All Scripture citations and references are from the New Revised Standard Version of the Bible. In some cases, I have shortened or paraphrased the NRSV text. To see the full version of these verses, look up the citations listed below.

1. *of the tradition.* 2 Corinthians 11:1-4.
2. *"to see Jesus."* John 12:20-21.
3. *the Baptizer.* John 1:19-28.

CHAPTER ONE

VAGABOND

The highway that winds up from the sea to Jerusalem is a rapidly ascending road through picturesque but rugged terrain. The heat is high and the vegetation sparse. Israeli military trucks lumber up the hill, making it slow going to the Holy City. Wrecks of tanks and rusting hulks from military skirmishes of the recent past have been left along the road as memorials to the fallen along this bloody, much disputed thoroughfare. The name Jerusalem means "foundation of peace," though it never lived up to its name. Stuck in fuming traffic, inching along in the heat, I muse, "What a road for God Almighty to walk."

Most people met Jesus on the road. When John the Baptizer introduced Jesus to the world, he quoted the prophet Isaiah, "Prepare the way of the Lord, make his paths straight. Every valley shall be filled, and every mountain and hill shall be made low . . . and all flesh shall see the salvation of God."[1] In Jesus, God worked a highway construction project, making a road straight through the desert to enslaved humanity. Just as in the exodus, when God made a "way" out of Egyptian slavery to the Promised Land,[2] so Jesus is the "way" to God.[3] How ironic that while we clamored up to God through our intellect, our morality, our architecture, our art, and our institutions (both secular and religious), in Jesus Christ, God slipped in among us. The first name for the church was simply "The Way,"[4] not only our way to God but rather God's way to us.

All the gospels present Jesus on a continual road trip—God in motion, urgently making a way to us in defeat of the desert in which we wander. *Euthys,* the Greek word for "immediately" occurs forty-two times in Mark's Gospel. No sooner does Jesus do something than "immediately" he hits the road to elsewhere. Some of Jesus' best words were spoken on the run. Many have wanted to know more about the early childhood and adolescence of Jesus. Matthew and Luke tell us a little about the circumstances of Jesus' birth, and Luke has one story about his going to the Temple in Jerusalem when he was twelve. In Mark, probably the earliest of the gospels, Jesus just shows up out of nowhere, gets baptized by John, and then the Spirit shoos him out into the wilderness. It is as if the gospels want to say that the action only really gets going when Jesus hits the road.

Jesus cannot be explained simply as the next chapter in the long, gradual, forward advance of humanity; his birth to a virgin named Mary signifies that Jesus is present as the miraculous gift of a gracious God, the God-given goal of all human history. The gospels tell us that knowing where this gift came from, who his people were, isn't going to help us much. If you want to know about Jesus, if you want to *know* him, you've got to meet him on the road.

What the gospels deem important about Jesus is not his family or his youth but rather his embarkation on his ministry, his forward movement, his mission. Breaking like a wave across dusty Galilee, he thunders forth into a captive land—God at highest momentum, God immediately. Anybody who wants to meet Jesus, to understand or be with Jesus, must be willing to relocate.

Aside to Jesus: At my advanced age, your frenetic pace is beginning to show on me. I long to locate, to bed down, settle in, and sit tight on what I already know of you rather than be forced to follow into some unknown destination. I find it remarkable that you have absolutely nothing to say about retirement. Have you found that you are at your best when working with people younger than thirty?

The Scriptures of Israel are a long story of how humanity busily attempts to be done with the God we have got. Shortly after God made us in God's own image,[5] we returned the compliment, trying to make God more palatable, someone who looked suspiciously like us. We so want to be gods unto ourselves. (The word *Israel* means "contend against God.") And yet in those same Scriptures, there is a sort of relentlessness about God's determination, despite our rebellion, to make a way toward Israel, to be God for us as God is, not as we would have God to be.

2

God promised to come in spite of our sad human history. God vowed to be with us, to show us God's glory, power, and love. That all sounded fine until God Almighty dramatically made good on the promise and actually showed up, not as the thoroughly malleable God we wanted but rather as Jesus of Nazareth. Even among Jesus' closest followers, his twelve disciples, there was this strange attraction to him combined with an understandable revulsion from him. "Blessed is anyone who takes no offense at me," he said.[6] But the things Jesus said and did led many to despise him. On a dark Friday afternoon in Jerusalem, that revulsion became bloody repulsion as we nailed Jesus' hands and feet to a cross and hoisted him up, naked, over a garbage dump outside of town. At last, we had silenced Jesus and the God he presented—or so we thought.

Three times, Jesus hinted that his death might not be the end of the drama,[7] yet the thought that anything in the world could be stronger than death was inconceivable to everyone around Jesus, even as it is inconceivable today. (Folks back then might not have known everything we know today, but they knew that what's dead stays dead.) All of his disciples were quickly resigned to his death. End of story. It was a good campaign while it lasted, but Jesus had not been enthroned as the national Messiah, the Savior of Israel. Caesar won. Rather than cry, "Crown him!" the crowd had screamed, "Crucify!" and stood by gleefully as the Romans nailed Jesus to a cross. Mocking him, the soldiers devised a crown of thorns and shoved it on his head, and they tacked above the cross a snide sign, "KING OF THE JEWS."[8] Some king, reigning from a cross. In about three hours, Jesus died of either suffocation or loss of blood, depending on whom you talk to.

As is so often the case with a true and living God, our sin was not the end of the story. Three days after Jesus had been brutally tortured to death by the government—egged on by a consortium of religious leaders like me, deserted by his disciples, and then entombed—a couple of his followers (women) went out in the predawn darkness to the cemetery.[9] The women went forth, despite the risk, to pay their last respects to the one who had publicly suffered the most ignominious of deaths. ("Where were the men who followed Jesus?" you ask. Let's just say for now that Jesus was never noted for the quality or courage of his male disciples.)

At the cemetery, place of rest and peace for the dead, the earth quaked. The huge stone placed before the tomb entrance (why on earth would the army need a big rock to keep the dead entombed?) was rolled away. An angel, messenger of God, perched impudently upon the rock.

The angel preached the first Easter sermon: "Don't be afraid. You seek Jesus, who was crucified? He is risen! Come, look at where he once lay in the tomb." Then the angel commissioned the women to be Jesus' first preachers: "Go, tell the men that he has already gone back to Galilee. There you will meet him."

It was a typically Jesus sort of moment, with people thinking they were coming close to where Jesus was resting, only to be told to "Go!" somewhere else. Jesus is God in motion, on the road, constantly going elsewhere, often to where he is not invited. Jesus was warned by his disciples not to go to Jerusalem, but Jesus, ever the bold traveler, did not let danger deter him, with predictable results—death on a cross. And now, on the first Easter morning, death doesn't daunt his mission. Jesus is once again on the move. So the angel says to the women, "You're looking for Jesus? Sorry, just missed him. By this time in the day, he's already in Galilee. If you are going to be with Jesus, get moving!"

The women obeyed and—sure enough—out in Galilee the risen Christ encountered them. Why Galilee? All of Jesus' disciples were Galileans. It's the Judean outback, a dusty, rural sort of place. Jesus himself hailed from Galilee, from Nazareth, a cheerless town in a forlorn region that swarmed with Gentiles. It was a notorious hotbed of Jewish resistance to Roman rule. ("Can anything good come out of Nazareth?" asked Nathaniel, before he met Jesus.[10])

So the risen Christ has returned once again to those who had so miserably forsaken and disappointed Jesus the first time around. It's emblematic of Jesus. Despite his disciples' betrayal, on the first day of his resurrected life, there's Jesus with nothing more pressing to do than immediately return to the ragtag group of Galilean losers who had failed him.

And what does Jesus say to them? Does he say, "You have all had a rough time lately. Settle down and snuggle in here in Galilee among these good country folks with whom you are most comfortable. Buy real estate, build a church, and enjoy being a spiritual club"? No, he doesn't say that. This is Jesus, after all, not a Methodist bishop. The risen Christ commands, "Get out of here! Make me disciples, baptizing, and teaching everything I've commanded you! And don't limit yourselves to Judea. Go to everybody. I'll stick with you until the end of time—just to be sure you obey me."[11]

How like peripatetic Jesus not to allow his people to rest, not to encourage them to hunker down with their own kind, but rather to send forth on the most perilous of missions those who had so disappointed him. They were, in Jesus' name, to go and take back the world that belonged to God. There is no way to be with Jesus, to love Jesus, without obeying Jesus, venturing with Jesus to "Go! Make disciples!"

By the way, in that time and in that place, the testimony of women was suspect, inadmissible in a court of law, ridiculed as worthless. So why would the early church have staked everything on the testimony of these women at the tomb? You can be sure that if the men (hunkered down in Jerusalem, I remind you) could have told the story of Jesus' resurrection another way, minus the women, they would have—which means that his earliest appearance to the women is exactly how it happened.

One expects the angel to say, "Don't be so sad," which is what we often say to people in grief. But the angel told the women, "Don't be afraid." When the resurrected Jesus met his disciples in Galilee, he said the same thing: "Don't be afraid!" One can understand why the dazzling angel at the empty tomb told the Roman guards not to be afraid.[12] After all, they had just been defeated by the resurrection of Jesus—perhaps it was payback time for Pontius Pilate. You would think the disciples would be glad that Jesus was raised from the dead and back with them. Why would the risen Christ need to command his followers not to fear?

Aside to Jesus: I must say that your propensity to work outside officially credentialed channels, to do what you do through people who are often considered to be the wrong age, gender, race, or social class is disturbing— particularly to many people in *my* gender, age, race, and social class.

I don't know for sure, but I think it was because it wasn't just, "Jesus is back from the dead!" nor much less (at least, at this point in the story), "Jesus is back from the dead, and we shall all live forever in heaven." Rather, it was, "*Jesus* has been raised from the dead!" Those who knew Jesus best, his disciples who had followed Jesus along the way from Galilee and who were now being sent by the risen Christ to the farthest reaches of the earth, knew enough about Jesus to realize that the angel's sermon, "He's back!" was not unadulterated good news. Furthermore, the risen Christ had just promised them, in effect, "I only had about three years to work on you and bring you face-to-face with the true God of Israel until the Romans caught up with me, but now I'm raised from the dead; I'm with you always, even to the end of the age! You will never, ever be rid of me!"

And thus were the disciples told, "Don't be afraid." Those who knew Jesus best, and were in turn known best by him, knew that, while friendship with Jesus is sweet, it is also demanding, difficult, and, at times, even fearsome.

As the Bible says, "It is a fearful thing to fall into the hands of the living God."[13] Presumably, it's not fearful to fall into the hands of a dead god, an idol who never shocks or demands anything of you, who is no more than a fake, a godlet, a mere projection of your fondest desires and silliest wishes. Out in Galilee—a dusty, drab, out-of-the-way sort of place, just like where most of us live—the disciples of Jesus were encountered by the living God. That Jesus could not only give death the slip but also be in Galilee suggests that the risen Christ could show up anywhere, anytime. And that's scary.

Here is God, not as a high-sounding principle, a noble ideal, or a set of rock-solid beliefs. Here is God on the move, moving toward us; God defined by God, God ordering us to be on the move into the world with God. And that's a joyful thing—but more than a little scary too. When it dawns on you that the living God is none other than Jesus of Nazareth, the Messiah we didn't expect, the Savior we didn't want, God in motion—well, fear is a reasonable reaction.

The modern world has many ways of turning us in on ourselves, eventually to worship the dear little god within. Christianity, the religion evoked by Jesus, is a decidedly fierce means of wrenching us outward. We are not left alone peacefully to console ourselves with our sweet bromides, or to snuggle with allegedly beautiful Mother Nature, or even to close our eyes and hug humanity in general. A God whom we couldn't have thought up on our own has turned to us, reached to us, is revealed to be someone quite other than the God we would have if God were merely a figment of our imagination—God is a Jew from Nazareth who lived briefly, died violently, and rose unexpectedly. This God scared us to death but also thrilled us to life. Why this mix of fear and joy was elicited by Jesus is one of the questions we'll be tackling in this book.

A few days after Jesus' resurrection, his followers figured out that they were caught up in some of that same death-to-life dynamic as Jesus. Paul told the church at Rome, "Therefore we have been buried with him by baptism into death, so that, just as Christ was raised from the dead by the glory of the Father, so we too might walk in newness of life."[14] And to the Ephesians, "God made us alive together with Christ . . . raised us up with him, made us to sit with him in heavenly places."[15] Living into resurrection, giving death the slip, they too were now on the move, just like Jesus. Jesus was, for them, not only the blinding light of the sun but also the fierce wind driving their lives where they would never have gone were they left to their own devices.

The Galilean who made fools of Death and of the Devil was a vagabond in many dimensions. The gospels differ on aspects of Jesus, but they agree that Jesus lived his adult life as a wandering beggar, without visible means of support. He never held a job or had a proper home. Many Jews expected God to come and save them; few expected God to show up as a homeless man, unmarried and unemployed. Constantly, Jesus crossed lines and transgressed boundaries. In clear violation of biblical law and custom, he reached out and touched lepers, insane persons, "unclean" women, corpses. Once, wandering about, he broke the law against plucking grain on the Sabbath, earning him the ire of the religious keepers of propriety.[16] His family thought he was mad. Some biblical authorities of the day attributed his healing powers to demonic possession.[17] He called the rich "fools,"[18] saying to them, "woe to you who are rich,"[19] and to the despised and neglected poor, he preached liberating "good news."[20] People like me, with advanced study in religion who made their living through interpreting God to less informed people like you, he called "whitewashed tombs," all spic and span outside, rotten inside.[21] Though he never had a cent, he often partied with tax collectors (the hated collaborators with the Roman occupation forces in Judea), and people despised him for it.[22] He praised the much hated Samaritans, making one a hero in a loved story.[23] In all these actions and in people's reactions, we see Jesus on the move, leading away from the status quo and toward some new, rather frightening realm called "the kingdom of God."

You can see why all the gospels depict Jesus as on a journey and those who believe in Jesus as fellow travelers. Any portrayal more static, fixed, and stable would be unfair to the subject. The gospels give us not definitions, explanations, and arguments but rather stories—beginning, middle, and end—that struggle to keep up with the movements of a living God. His way was more than a line on a map, certainly more than a one-way street to heaven. His way is not only the route he took but the way he walked and talked, as well as the way he died. And the way he rose. Most important of all, he *is* the way.

> Aside to Jesus: I hope you see these paragraphs as being incredibly generous of me—affluent, foolish, whitewashed entombed defender of the status quo though I am.

Vagabond Jesus went from place to place healing, teaching, finding food and shelter wherever it was proffered. He told his followers to take no money, food, or protective staff, to be totally dependent on the kindness of strangers. They were not to be impeded with the baggage that the world considers necessary.[24] Something about Jesus led these ordinary folks to forsake everything and follow.[25] Those whom he chose as disciples appear to have had little formal organization, no material resources, save those kept by the traitor Judas, and not much talent for being revolutionaries. Looking at his life and legacy, it's no wonder that many then and now regard him as a well-intentioned but sadly deluded failure.

And yet the Letter to the Hebrews says that this homeless, begging, crucified vagabond is "the reflection of God's glory and the exact imprint of God's very being." [26]

Sometimes people say, "God? Oh, can't say anything definitive about God. God is large, nebulous, and vague." We wish. By rendering God into an abstract idea, we can be assured that we'll always be safe from God. By raising the crucified Jesus from the dead, it was as if God vindicated Jesus, as if God said, "You want to know what God looks like? You want to know what the Creator really wants from the creature and creation? Look at Jesus! There, that's who I am." At a definite point in time, at a particular place, in love, God allowed God's self to be pinned down by us—on a cross. It's a curious thing to say about Jesus, the wandering teacher of Galilee, that he is as much of God as we ever hope to see. Even more so, Jesus is a curious thing to say about God.

It wasn't simply that, "God has raised a person from the dead." Who would have gotten worked up over, "God has raised Julius Caesar from the dead"? Rather, the Christian message was, "God raised *Jesus* from the dead." God raised this one who forgave his enemies, who reached out to the sinner and the outcast, who stood up to the authorities, and who invited everyone to his kingdom. That One is raised.

Not only was he on the move but also Jesus constantly invited everyone to join his journey. In my pastoral experience, Jesus holds little interest for people who are at ease with themselves here, now, in this place, living their lives as the world tells them, content as pigs in mud. Jesus tends to come to people where they are but rarely leaves them as they were. Conversion of thought and life, a whole new world, is part of the adventure of being loved by Jesus, of being invited to be his traveling companion. Thus, the writer to the church at Ephesus exclaimed, "If any one is in Christ—new creation!"[27] That's bad news for those who are complacent with the world as it is; good news for those who think that they may have been created for more than merely present arrangements.

On the day of resurrection, John's Gospel says that Mary Magdalene went by herself in the dark to the tomb of Jesus.[28] (You already know that the male disciples weren't with her.) She peered in the tomb and, to her horror, saw that, apparently, in one last ignominious act, somebody

> Aside to Jesus: Here, let me thank you that, through the church, you have introduced me to lots of folks for whom the world has not been as comfortable, good, and seductive as the world has been to me and my family, adamant that I take responsibility for them and their needs, referring to these strangers as "brother" and "sister."

had swiped the body of Jesus. At least, that's what she thought. Mary went back to town to summon the slumbering men. Later that morning, Mary was again outside Jesus' empty tomb, weeping. She was startled by a man standing beside her. The man asked why she wept. Mary presumed that he was a gardener for the cemetery. Then the stranger called her name, "Mary." And she joyfully exclaimed, "Rabbi!"

When she hugged Jesus he said, "Don't hold on to me, I'm ascending to my Father and your Father, to my God and your God."[29]

How like the wild vagabond whom Mary loved. "Don't try to pin me down," he seemed to say. The Traveler who had come from God was now "ascending," returning to God, as the resurrected one. The one who had come from the Father had, in his words and work, revealed to his followers that God is more than great, better than good; God is *"your* Father," *"your* God." And yet, though he loved his disciples like Mary, the Vagabond would not be restrained, constrained, or contained. He was now free not only from death but also from the limits those who loved him might attempt to impose upon him.

That's why Christian thought and doctrine is never final, finished, and static. God is alive, in motion toward us, in movement beyond us, not only two thousand years ago but now. Jesus is a journey. It's probably a good thing for believers in Jesus to maintain a degree of modesty and tentativeness in what we claim to know about Jesus. If he is who the Scriptures say that he is, we'll never completely grasp him, for he is bigger than our ability to hold fully on to him. He holds on to us.

The Bible introduces us to a living, speaking, moving Person, not to the fixed and final word on everything. I'll confess that something in me would like to tell you that you can't really come to Jesus if you don't come through my presentation of Jesus, preferably as a dues-paying member of my particular church. But then I recall this episode with Jesus and Mary Magdalene, and I hear Jesus say to me, not to you, "Don't hold me! I'm on the move!" Vagabond Jesus won't be held down by me in his determination to move freely toward you.

John begins his rollicking gospel account of Jesus by taking Jesus to, of all places, a post-wedding bash in Cana, where Jesus shows up with twelve unattached men.[30] During the merriment, the wine ran out. Mary, mother of Jesus, implored him to revive the rapidly wilting party. At first, Jesus brushes her off with, "Woman, what does that have to do with you or me? It's not my party. My hour has not yet come."

Of course it's not Jesus' hour; it's only the second chapter of the Gospel. But then Jesus tells the manager of the feast to fill up six stone jars with 180 gallons of water. Miraculously, the water is turned to premium wine. There is more than enough alcohol for the most memorable of all Judean parties. I love to tell this story to those who think that Christianity is mostly a matter of dos and don'ts or an ethically rigorous program to help you "live a better life." The wedding at Cana (like many Jesus stories) resists our utilization for any purpose other than being weird with Jesus.

John comments that this was "the first of his signs." A sign of what? A sign that Jesus should go into catering? A sign that Jesus had violated policy prohibiting alcohol at church-sponsored social events?

Furthermore, John says that his twelve disciples "believed in him." Some saw "glory." What on earth did they believe? And where's the glory? Jesus has, up to this point, done no teaching or preaching and has asked no one to believe anything about him. Yet some believe; they want to follow Jesus toward this strange, useless glory. Sometimes people believe Jesus, love Jesus, and follow Jesus on the basis of less than adequate information or evidence. It's the effect Jesus has on some. Is he having that effect on you?

They get to know Jesus only by catching some brief, enigmatic whiff of his glory and stumbling after. Then,

> Aside to Jesus: I hope you appreciate how this story about your antics at the wedding party made my work with college students much more difficult. When I was hammering on one student for his abuse of alcohol on campus, he, being a Baptist, shot back with, "At least I didn't go as far as Jesus went in John 2."

without suitable explanation or moralistic instruction, Jesus left Cana. He wandered elsewhere, surely leaving many believers and unbelievers alike (on their way to sleep off the 180 gallons of wine) scratching their heads and asking, "Why Jesus?"

YOU CAN LOOK IT UP

1. *"salvation of God."* Matthew 3:4-6 quoting Isaiah 40:3-5.

2. *the Promised Land*, Isaiah 30:21; 35:8; 40:3.

3. *"way" to God.* John 14:6.

4. *"The Way,"* Acts 9:2.

5. *God's own image*, Genesis 1:26-27.

6. *"at me,"* he said. Matthew 11:6.

7. *of the drama.* Mark 8:31; 9:31; 10:34.

8. *"OF THE JEWS."* Matthew 27:37.

9. *to the cemetery.* Matthew 28:1-10.

10. *he met Jesus.* John 1:46.

11. *"you obey me."* Matthew 28:16-20.

12. *not to be afraid.* Matthew 28:4.

13. *"the living God."* Hebrews 10:31.

14. *"newness of life."* Romans 6:4.

15. *"heavenly places."* Ephesians 2:5-6.

16. *keepers of propriety.* Matthew 12:1 ff.

17. *to demonic possession.* Mark 3:22.

18. *the rich "fools,"* Luke 12:20.

19. *"you who are rich,"* Luke 6:24.

20. *liberating "good news."* Luke 4:18.

21. *rotten inside.* Matthew 23:27.

22. *despised him for it.* Luke 5:29-30.

23. *loved story.* Luke 9:51-56; 10:33; 17:11-19.

24. *world considers necessary.* Luke 10:4.

25. *everything and follow.* Luke 18:28.

26. *"God's very being."* Hebrews 1:3.

27. *"new creation!"* 2 Corinthians 5:17.

28. *tomb of Jesus.* John 20:11 ff.

29. *"and your God."* John 20:17.

30. *twelve unattached men.* John 2:1-10.

CHAPTER TWO

PEACEMAKER

I haven't come to bring peace but a sword," he thundered. "I've come to turn father against son, mother against daughter."[1] He who never raised a sword, even in self defense, nor permitted his disciples to carry or to use swords, openly proclaimed his message as a "sword."

"I came to bring fire to the earth. . . . Do you think that I have come to bring peace to the earth? No, I tell you, but rather division!"[2] So when Christians acclaim Jesus as the "Prince of Peace," we use *prince* and *peace* in ways that are patently peculiar. Jesus brings peace, but his peace often begins as disruption and despair before it is sensed as peace. It is not peace as the world gives, his peace.[3] Prince of Peace Jesus was a threat to world peace.

Prince of Peace Jesus never backed off from an argument, never scurried away from a howling mob or confrontation with a scathing critic. He "taught with authority," meaning that he knew the Bible better than the scribes and Pharisees (who quoted Scripture to Jesus more than he quoted it to them). The religious leaders backed up their arguments with Jesus by quoting the authority of Scripture—never admitting that their assertions were based on their opinions or social custom. Jesus spoke with authority that was personal: "you have heard it said, but I tell you . . ." He made a scandalous move from saying "we have always believed" to "But I say to you that . . ." As his critics noted, nobody ought to talk so subversively and disruptively—unless he is God.

Back in the Old Testament, Israel's King Ahaz had a big problem. The murderous Assyrians were at his doorstep, and Ahaz feared that he lacked the army to withstand them. National security was code orange. King Ahaz summoned his court chaplain, the prophet Isaiah. "Help!" pleaded Ahaz.[4] "Give me a sign that God will be with us in this battle."

Isaiah (Jesus' favorite prophet, by the way) responded sonorously, "Behold, a virgin will conceive and bear a son, and his name will be called Emmanuel, that is, God-with-us."

Ahaz surely responded, "I ask for a sign of victory, and all you can come up with is a baby? I need chariots, warriors, a dependable army—not a baby!" Matthew remembered that obscure moment when he retold the story of Jesus' conception.

At Jesus' birth, according to Luke, the sky filled with a battalion of angels, all singing, "Glory to God in the Highest and on earth peace to those with whom God is well pleased."[5] Shepherds—poor people, nobodies working the night shift—alone heard the royal angelic proclamation. They scurried to Bethlehem to meet the new king. The "king" they found was a defenseless baby lying in a manger. That's God's great answer to what's wrong with the world? A baby born to an unwed mother? An infant wrapped in rags, cast into a cattle feed trough?

The announcement, "Glory to God in the Highest and on earth peace," is an almost direct quote from the prelude to Caesar's royal proclamations that were read in the marketplace in the occupied territories whenever the emperor wanted something done. "Glory to Augustus Caesar, God in the Highest, and on earth, peace to those with whom he is well pleased," (and presumably hell on earth to those with whom Caesar is not pleased). See what Luke is doing? The angels' song is not only a birth announcement; it's a war chant, a proclamation announcing a change of government. There is a new king in town, and Caesar's rule is imperiled. Again Isaiah: The government is being placed upon the shoulders of a baby.[6]

Which is the main reason why Matthew says that, when the visiting magi told King Herod (the Jewish lackey assisting in the Roman occupation of Jerusalem) that a new "king" had been born in Bethlehem, "He was troubled, and all Jerusalem with him."[7]

"We already have a king—me," Herod must have said to these visiting Iraqis. Troubled Herod reacted in the usual royal way, by ordering a massacre of all the Jewish boy babies (the way kings deal with threats to their sovereignty), one of the many Gentile pogroms against God's beloved people. Now, can you understand why nobody ever put Matthew's bloody account of the nativity on a Christmas card? We like our nativities sweetly sentimental rather than so blatantly political.

My point is that, from the beginning, Jesus was a cause of much violence and bloodshed, though none of it was initiated by him. Jesus came to an Israel that was a political and military weakling, defeated, under the heel of Rome. But Jews didn't take this heavy-handed rule sitting down. There were dozens of uprisings against their military masters. Those in power, like Herod, were smart enough to see in Jesus a political challenge, and they responded accordingly. Two thousand Jews were crucified about the time of Jesus' birth after they had launched a raid on the Roman arsenal at Sepphoris, a prosperous town not far from Nazareth. Jesus knew exactly what the Romans did to Jews who threatened their lordship.

Even "all Jerusalem" knew that the angels' good news was not unadulteratedly good. The uneasy peace that had been worked out with Rome was threatened. And most people love law and order more than the laws of God. Though the announcing angel had told Mary and Joseph to call their baby Joshua, or Jesus, meaning "God saves" (Joshua had led the conquering Israelites into the promised land[8]), the name Jesus meant nothing but trouble for the governing authorities and all those who profited from the "peace" that the army had imposed.

Mary had a peaceful life—until God stepped in. When an angel visited her at the inception, Mary was let in on the secret. In response, Mary sang a song that was no sweet lullaby: God is at last moving to liberate God's people, but not necessarily in a way that was expected. The poor, the marginalized, those on the bottom, are being moved up, given "good things." The rich, those who have enjoyed relative security and prosperity in present arrangements, are going to descend, be divested, dethroned, and sent away empty.[9]

"Lord, will you at this time restore the kingdom to Israel?"[10] Jesus' disciples asked after his resurrection. That is, "Lord, will you at this time finally act like a Messiah, mount your war horse, raise a royal army, rout our Roman occupiers, and set up Israel as the nation we are meant to be?"

Christ meant "Messiah," which means the Anointed, the king, the political/military hero. Politics is power, our only means of transcending the problems of this world. "Jesus, when are you at last going to move from spiritual blather to something important—like politics?" Jesus responded by telling his followers that it was not for them to know the times for such things. Jesus seems somewhat evasive, reluctant to come right out and say,

"I'm the Messiah you have been expecting," probably because he knew that their messianic expectations were not for someone like him.

> Aside to Jesus: How much easier you would be for us to take if we could regard you as of mainly "spiritual" significance. We get nervous when you push into politics. Politics has become for us the functional equivalent of God, our protector from cradle to grave, the source of security, the only means of doing any good in the world, the sole subject of Fox News. How much easier for us to keep you private and personal rather than public and political.

At this point, honesty compels me to say that, if you are one of those people with great love for the government or reverent respect for the military that props up government, you will find Jesus a jolt to your sensibilities. The modern state—with its flags, pronouncements, parades, propaganda, public works projects, and assorted patriotic paraphernalia—does not mesh well with Jesus. Patriotism, while perhaps a virtue, has never been regarded as a specifically Christian virtue.

In truth, Jesus was very "political," but not as we expected. After his arrest—by functionaries of the state—Jesus stood before Pontius Pilate, who was seated upon the judgment seat to render a verdict on Jesus.[11]

"So, are you king?" asked Pilate, sarcasm dripping from his urbane Roman lips. Jesus responded, "You have said so," implying that much of this concern about royalty and authority was Pilate's preoccupation, not his. Then Jesus pronounced, "My kingdom is not of this world," or at least, that's how his words are sometimes translated. Closer to the Greek: "My kingdom is not from here."[12]

It's a mistake to interpret Jesus as having said, "My kingdom is out of this world, something otherworldly, spiritual even." Rather, Jesus is saying, "My kingdom is not from here, here with all these royal trappings and raw power, here propped up with swords and acting as if it were from God. My reign is not secured by the swords of Caesar's finest. My authority derives from elsewhere."

16

And then Jesus commented that if his kingdom were "from here," established by the powers that sustain earthly kingdoms, his followers would march and make war on Pilate's kingdom. Jesus' followers do not take up the sword because they are citizens of a kingdom "not from here."

And slowly in the conversation, power subtly shifts from this presumed powerful Roman bureaucrat, Pontius Pilate, to the seemingly bedraggled, whipped, and bound Jew before him. Pilate, and all that he represents, is being judged by the prisoner whom Pilate thought he was judging. Jesus, as strange a "king" as ever there was, is judgment upon our definitions of monarchy. Thus, Jesus had made a subversive nuisance of himself to all Pilate's successors.

On the night a squad of soldiers arrested him, Jesus mocked them, undaunted, asking if they were armed to the teeth to arrest him, an unarmed rabbi, as if he were a common thief.[13] Ironically, the soldiers were not the only ones with swords. Peter, the most impetuous of Jesus' disciples, the "rock" upon which Jesus promised to build his church, whipped out a sword and nicked off a bit of an ear—despite Jesus' clear commandment that his disciples not carry weapons.[14] Jesus cursed Peter: "Those who take up the sword die by the sword." That night, Jesus once again refused to practice violence, even in self-defense.

"Those who take up the sword die by the sword" is one of the truest proverbs of Jesus. Both the victor and the vanquished must finally submit to the power of the sword. The sword we thought we were using to secure ourselves becomes our ultimate defeat.

As everybody knows, there is no way to get anything really important done without swords. That's why we have the largest military budget of any nation in the world—to achieve security and then preemptively to spread peace and freedom everywhere. What war has been waged except from the very best of motives? To call Jesus a "Prince of Peace" is an oxymoron. A political leader who doesn't make war when national security is threatened is no prince. And peace that is based on anything other than a balance of military power is inconceivable.

Thus, one of the most perennially confusing qualities of Jesus was his refusal of violence. "If someone slaps you on the right cheek, offer them your left cheek as well. Some Roman soldier commands, 'Jew, carry my backpack a mile,' take it one mile more.[15] Pray for your enemies! Bless those who persecute you! Do not resist the evil one!" As if to underscore that his kingdom was "not from here," Jesus healed the daughter of a despised Roman centurion.[16] Was this any way to establish a new kingdom?

It would have been amazing enough if Jesus had said, "I always turn the other cheek when someone wrongs me," or "I refuse to return violence when violence is done to me."[17] After all, Jesus is the Son of God, and we expect him to be nice. Unfortunately, Jesus commanded his disciples—us, those who presumed to follow him—to behave nonviolently. How do we get back at our enemies? "Love your enemies!"[18] What are we to do when we are persecuted for following Jesus? "Pray for those who persecute you."[19] Thus, we have many instances in the New Testament of people violating and killing the followers of Jesus. But we have not one single instance of any of his followers defending themselves against violence, except for Peter's inept, rebuked attempt at sword play.

> Aside to Jesus: It's amazing that you told your disciples there was a cross awaiting not only you but them as well. What a sales pitch! "Follow me—and be crucified!"

This consistent, right-to-the-end, to-the-point-of-death nonviolence of Jesus has been that which Jesus' followers have most attempted to modify. When it comes to violence in service of a good cause, we deeply wish Jesus had said otherwise. There are many rationales for the "just war," or for self-defense, capital punishment, abortion, national security, or military strength. None of them, you will note, is able to make reference to Jesus or to the words or deeds of any of his first followers. You can argue that violence is sometimes effective, or justified by the circumstances, or a possible means to some better end, or practiced by every nation on the face of the earth—but you can't drag Jesus into the argument with you. This has always been a source of annoyance and has provoked some fancy intellectual footwork on the part of those who desire to justify violence. Sorry, Jesus just won't cooperate.

Today, some critics charge religion with being the source of humanity's worst violence. This is a ruse perpetuated by those who unthinkingly lump Jesus with "religion" and who are (probably unknowingly) attempting to exonerate the pretentious modern nation-state from its role as the source of the worst violence the world has ever seen. The modern nation, democratic or otherwise, the modern functional equivalent of God, has proved to be the bloodiest concoction ever invented by a presumptuous humanity.

Though certain religious leaders, some of them even claiming to follow Jesus, have various rationales for commending violence, Jesus never once reacted violently to his critics and crucifiers; in fact, he forgave them. There is not one single instance of Jesus—or of any of his followers in the entire New Testament—commending the use of force. How Jesus got dragged into this bloody mess is testimony to how little people know about Jesus and how unfaithful the church has been in following him.

The thoroughgoing, unqualified nonviolence of Jesus has always been a reproach to those of us who think of Jesus as the full revelation of God, particularly for people like me, from South Carolina, for whom violence is natural. How on earth could Jesus contend that the kingdom of God could be reached through peacefulness, forgiveness, and nonviolent means? A clue may lie in Jesus' beloved "Sermon on the Mount."[20] There, after Jesus commends going the second mile, turning the other cheek, forgiving enemies, and blessing those who persecute us for his sake, Jesus says that we are to be "perfect as your Father in heaven is perfect." There, is that too difficult?

Jesus, in the Sermon on the Mount, commends nonviolence, nonretaliation, and forgiveness, not on the basis of effectiveness, not from some silly notion that if we forgive our enemies, it is sure to bring out the best in them, but rather because this is the way of "your Father in heaven." Peacefulness is the way God is. Despite what you have been told by your politicians ("Might makes right," "this is the way of national security," "capital punishment is a deterrence for crime," "we had to invade the country in order to give them freedom," "abortion is a matter of freedom of choice," and so forth), reality is otherwise. At the heart of the universe is not dog-eat-dog, survival-of-the-fittest struggle and war. At the heart of it all is a God who is peaceful, loving, long-suffering, forgiving, and gracious. Jesus looks like God; God looks like Jesus. We need not take matters in hand and fix the world with the only means we know—bloodshed. God will fix things with this Jew from Nazareth who refused to fight back and who died not threatening, "One day, damn you, I'll get even," but rather praying, "Father, forgive."

Of course, we would have known none of this about God, about reality, and about the world if it were not for Jesus. Thus, the answer to, "Why

Jesus?" is the same as the answer to the question, "What's really going on in the world?"

What's really going on is made manifest in Jesus. Though he did not, at first, impress us as the Messiah (by refusing to live up to our expectations of what a messiah is), eventually, some got the point and worshiped him. They adored him, not necessarily as the means to a better world, not as an effective catalyst for social change, but rather as the way God really is, all the way down. He is reality, and in him, we see that reality is peace. True, it is a peace "that passes all understanding."[21] It is not peace that one achieves by studying the course of world history or by meditating upon the human condition. His peace comes as a gift from the one who is known, paradoxically, as the Prince of Peace, the clue to what's really going on in the world, the revelation of who God really is.

So Jesus hangs upon a bloody cross, humiliated before the whole world. The mob taunts, "If you are really tight with God, command your legions of angels to take charge, to come down and defeat your enemies and deliver you."

But Jesus just hanged there. He breathed his last, and he died. This is the way God's kingdom comes? This is the way God wins victory? A stupendous claim, not made before or since by any religion: God not only takes the side of the innocent victim of violence and injustice but becomes one of them.

Jesus advocated no systematic program of human reform, never recommended any collective social adjustments, no matter how badly needed or enlightened. Jesus was not big on ethical codes, had no ideology, did no interesting work in political science or social ethics, and never put forth a plan of action, other than the (seemingly) wildly impractical notions that the first will be last, that we must turn the other cheek to those who strike us, and that we should become like little children.

Likewise, Jesus appears to have had no interest in one of the world's great, abiding illusions—justice. At various times, Jesus was dragged before the agents of justice—Caiaphas (the high priest), the Sanhedrin, Pontius Pilate (Jesus made little distinction between religious power brokers and secular ones). One of the most noble systems of justice ever devised responded to Jesus by torturing him to death. Worldly attempts at justice always involve the strong imposing their wills upon the weak. In crying for justice, the weak are usually demanding power to work their wills upon the strong. Perhaps that's why, in world history, Jesus is usually on the losing side. After the world's revolutions, it's often difficult to tell the vanquished from the victors, morally speaking. People in power tend to act the same, despite why they got there. All of which explains why Jesus never got along well with potentates, religious or otherwise.

Once, when Peter asked Jesus for a coin to pay the requisite temple tax, Jesus rather flippantly told the big fisherman to go catch a fish and pull the tax money out of the fish's mouth.[22] There is no record that Peter actually went and did so, which makes me wonder if Jesus was serious. Perhaps Jesus was saying that we owe the governing authorities not much more than can be expectorated out of the mouth of a fish. I take this story as yet another indication of the shockingly nonchalant way that Jesus dealt with affairs of state.

Surely, this is why Jesus was more comprehensible to the simple than to the sophisticated. (Once, he prayed to his Father, giving thanks that his truth was hidden to the reputedly wise.[23]) When a couple of his disciples got into an argument over who was the greatest in the kingdom of God, he rebuked them, telling them that one entered his kingdom by being reduced to the level of a child.[24] This is good news because the big people—the Herods, Pontius Pilates, and the Wall Street tycoons—have a way of eventually making the people under them feel very small, needy, and vulnerable. Jesus preached the good news that God's kingdom has a very small door, right-sized for the lowly to enter, so low that big people are required to stoop.

Few of us exercise political clout. Our power arises not from our political beliefs but rather from our material possessions. Most of us in the West live on a scale that, in Jesus' day, could be attained only by the likes of Herod. It is doubtful that Jesus would be any easier on us than he was on Herod (whom he insolently referred to as "that fox"[25]). "You cannot love God and money," he said flatly.[26]

> Aside to Jesus: OK, let's be honest: when we don't want to follow you, it's not because we don't yet have enough information about you or can't swallow what the gospels say about you. No, our reservations are due to the cars we drive and the houses in which we live.

To be poor, old, disabled, or young is to be without power. Violence is the provenance of the powerful; it's the way the world gets good things done. The poor know what it means to be without means, without security, or without hope in their own resources. They gladly heard Jesus.

I've just returned from Haiti: they still joyfully hear Jesus.

Jesus was often called "rabbi," that is, "teacher." Yet I know of no teacher who demanded so much of his students. He desired not only that his disciples agree with his ideas but also follow his narrow way—turning the other cheek, not remarrying after divorce, not accumulating material things. That which we regard as the very goal of life, Jesus dismisses as deleterious baggage.

One day while he was on the road, a well-to-do young adult asked Jesus, "What must I do to inherit eternal life?"[27] For one who received so much of his present status through inheritance, it was a logical question. Also, because he heard that Jesus was a rabbi, it was understandable that he asked Jesus a fuzzy, rather religious-sounding question about the sweet by and by. When Mark tells this story, Mark says that, "Jesus looked at him and loved him"[28] and said, "Go sell all that you have and give the proceeds to the poor. Then, follow me." (Do you really want to be loved by Jesus?)

With that, the young man slumped down, got depressed, and left, leaving Jesus to mutter, "How hard it is for those with riches to enter the kingdom of God." It is the only time in the gospels that Jesus invited someone to be a disciple and the person refused. And the reason was money.

"How hard is it?" the disciples whined.

"It is easier to shove a fully loaded dromedary through the eye of a needle than for a Wall Street investment banker to get into the kingdom of God. Still, even something that outlandish (the salvation of the rich) just may occur since with God, all things are . . . possible." Salvation in Jesus' name requires divestment.

Jesus appears never to have carried a cent of cash. He expressed not simply disapproval but downright scorn for people who did. When he sent his disciples out to do their work, he told them to take no purses or even an extra pair of shoes, to rely solely upon God for their security.[29] Jesus thus made money a God issue.

One day, Jesus' critics, seeking to entrap him, asked, "Ought we pay taxes to Caesar?"[30] It was a trick. If Jesus says, "yes, pay taxes," it will make him

22

a collaborator with the Roman occupiers. If he says, "no," he could risk the Romans' wrath.

Instead, Jesus asks, "Who has a coin?" (His pockets are empty.) A coin is produced. "Whose image is stamped on the coin?"

"Caesar's," is the reply.

Jesus answers, "Then give to Caesar what is Caesar's; but you take care to give to God what is God's."

End of discussion. Did someone protest, "But you didn't answer the question, Jesus; just what is God's and what is Caesar's?" No, because the answer is self-evident. Every Jew knew by heart the words, "the earth is the Lord's and everything in it."[31] They also knew the Genesis claim that each of us is stamped "in the image of God."[32] Not much is left for Caesar to rule after such sweeping claims for the proprietorship of God.

Thus, Jesus, good, contentious Jew that he was, takes a discussion about the propriety of paying taxes to Caesar and frames it as a debate about the First Commandment. We are not permitted to bow to other gods. Every day the orthodox Jew must jump out of bed and learn again to "monotheize," to place absolutely nothing in the way of the worship of the one, true, only living God. Every time Christians worship "in Jesus' name," examination of our possible idolatries is our main business. Why Jesus? Why must other-wise potentially good things like our nation or our money be called into question? Why must some of our most widely held and cherished values be considered as possible diversions from worship of God?

Jesus answers with his words and his life. When asked about the greatest of all the commandments, Jesus gave a very Jewish answer, "Hear, O Israel, the Lord your God is one; and you shall love the Lord your God with all your heart, and with all your soul, and with all your mind, and with all your strength." In other words, the Lord God is not only one, but the one and only. To this Jesus added a second from Leviticus 19:18: "You shall love your neighbor as yourself."[33]

In order to get neighbor love right, we must get God right. Love of God in Jesus Christ is rationale for love of neighbor as child of God. We can't call God "Father," as Jesus taught us to pray, without calling our neighbor "sister," "brother." However, there is an admittedly exclusive implication to this otherwise inclusive stance toward the world. We see it in Jesus' repeated warnings about the danger of idolatry. We cannot love God with everything we've got if we are preoccupied with love of God's chief competitors. We will never love the neighbor if we deify the state, for the state is what teaches us to regard our neighbors across the border as potential threats, as enemies. We are able to love only one Lord at a time. To believe that Jesus is God, that this wandering Jew from Nazareth is Savior of the world, God reconciling the world to God, is also to disbelieve that anyone or anything else can be.

Jesus said, "Peace I give to you, but not as the world gives peace."

I'll say.

YOU CAN LOOK IT UP

1. *"mother against daughter."* Matthew 10:35.
2. *"but rather division!"* Luke 12:49-51.
3. *his peace.* John 14:27.
4. *"Help!" pleaded Ahaz.* Isaiah 7.
5. *"is well pleased."* Luke 2:13-14.
6. *of a baby.* Isaiah 7:14.
7. *"Jerusalem with him."* Matthew 2:3.
8. *the promised land.* Joshua 1-4.
9. *sent away empty.* Luke 1:53.
10. *"kingdom to Israel?"* Acts 1:6.
11. *verdict on Jesus.* John 19.
12. *"not from here."* John 18:36.
13. *a common thief.* Mark 14:48.
14. *not carry weapons.* Luke 22:49-51.
15. *one mile more.* Matthew 5:41.
16. *a Roman centurion.* Matthew 8:5.
17. *"done to me."* Matthew 5:39.
18. *"Love your enemies!"* Luke 6:35.
19. *"who persecute you."* Matthew 5:44.
20. *"Sermon on the Mount."* Matthew 5.
21. *"passes all understanding."* Philippians 4:7.
22. *the fish's mouth.* Matthew 17:27.
23. *the reputedly wise.* Luke 10:21.
24. *level of a child.* Mark 10:15.
25. *"that fox."* Luke 13:32.
26. *he said flatly.* Matthew 19:16 ff.
27. *"inherit eternal life?"* Luke 18:18.
28. *"loved him,"* Mark 10:21.
29. *for their security.* Luke 10:4.
30. *"taxes to Caesar?"* Matthew 22:19 ff.
31. *"everything in it."* Psalm 24:1.
32. *"image of God."* Genesis 1:26.
33. *"as yourself."* Mark 12:31.

CHAPTER THREE

STORYTELLER

Once upon a time, there was a rich man (and you know how we despise the rich) who got word that his manager was pilfering from him.[1] So he summoned the little guy for an audit.

"What's this I hear? Show me the books!"

"Er, Boss, uh, nothin' would please me more than to show you the books—I need to do a few . . . calculations."

The little weasel thinks to himself, "I'm too proud to beg and too weak to do any real work. What am I to do? I've got it! I'll call in my master's debtors and have them write down their debts. They'll be so grateful that, when my master sacks me, I can go to them for help."

Thus, the swindle begins. Each of the debtors is called in and asked, "You owe the master $1,000? Let's mark that down to $250. How you like them numbers?"

Huge sums of money are written off.

Then comes the day of judgment. Now the little wretch will get what his thievery deserves. The dishonest manager presents the cooked books to the master. The master responds with, "You . . . you *genius* you! Wow! What wonderful initiative. What commercial creativity. What innovative book keeping. I wish all my people were as smart in looking after their future."

Now, what kind of Savior would have told a story like that to people like us? (Yep, he really did tell this story.)[2]

Did you hear the one about the man traveling from Jerusalem to Jericho who was mugged, beaten, stripped naked, and left to die like a dog in a ditch?[3]

Now, by chance, down the road comes a priest, a religious official, a man who makes his living off of God—and you know how we all despise clergy. He espies the man bleeding, lying helpless in the ditch, and the priest . . . passes by on the other side.

Then comes down the road a pious but not priggish, religious but not showy, ordinary Methodist person who, catching a whiff of the now putrefying mess in the ditch—and being religious and therefore quite a cautious sort of person—passes by on the other side.

Imagine you are the man in the ditch. You've lost a lot of blood. Time is running out. With your last ounce of energy you look down that hot, dusty road and see coming toward you—a nice-looking, spiritual but not fanatical, probably Republican, traditional-values person like you? No. You see a despised, good-for-nothing, racially impure, theologically uninformed *Samaritan.* Your last best hope is a man whom you hate.

And despite your weak protests—"it's only a flesh wound. I'm OK, I'm OK"—this lousy Samaritan rips up his designer suit, lays your bleeding carcass on the fine leather seats of his Porsche, takes you to the hospital, shells out all of his credit cards, and tells them to spare no expense in your salvation.

"Go and do likewise," says Jesus.

Is this a joke? Parables, these pithy, strange little stories from everyday life, are the most distinctive—and peculiar—aspect of the teaching of Jesus. Parables are close cousins of another distinctive literary form: the joke. Mark says that Jesus never said anything in public that wasn't a parable.[4] There are religious teachers who, when asked a theological question, respond with thoughtful, general principles, high-sounding, serious and uplifting. Muhammad and Dr. Phil McGraw leap to mind.

Why, Jesus? Why do you explain God with unexplained stories, most of which lack neat endings or immediately apparent points? It's as if Jesus says that God is not met through generalities and abstractions; God is met amid the stuff of daily life, in the tug and pull of the ordinary. Yet God is usually encountered, if the parables have it right, in ways that are rarely self-evident, obvious, or with uncontested meaning. In parables, the joke is on us.

What is God like? A dragnet is thrown into the sea.[5] When the net is hauled in, it bristles with all sorts of creatures, a few good fish but lots of trash as well. The servants ask, "Master, do you want us to sort the good fish from the bad?"

"No, let's worry about the culling on another day. What a huge haul!"

God is like that. There, now. Are there other questions?

Don't be troubled if you can't figure out that story; the disciples who first heard it didn't get it either. Jesus comes across at times as this Zen-like teacher whose greatest desire is not to pass out the right answers but rather to tease and to provoke even more questions. I'm sure that it comes as little surprise that a frequent response to his parables was befuddlement. Perhaps Jesus was attempting to talk about matters (God, the kingdom of God) that can't be simply explicated without damaging the truth of what he was trying to talk about. Perhaps what Jesus was trying to do in his parables was more than make a point. Perhaps mere intellectual understanding was not the point.

> Aside to Jesus: I confess that I'm guilty of thinking that God is somewhat like me, only nicer. God thinks like me when I'm having a really good day. I love the way your parables push me to admit, "Wow, I guess I really don't know God."

A frustrated farmer is stuck with a woefully inept fig tree.[6] Three years, no figs. In Judea, fig trees bear fruit twice every year. But this tree has never borne fruit.

"Cut it down!" says the owner. Time's up for this worthless tree.

But a servant pleads, "Master, let it alone (Greek: *aphetes,* which also can mean "forgive it"). I'll dig around it, pile on manure (Greek: *koprion,* which also means "dung," "feces," or worse), and then, let's see what happens, and you can do as you please."

God is that way.

On his way to Jerusalem, Jesus throws out an even more curt parable when he asks, if a homeowner had known at what hour a thief would break in, do you think the homeowner would have slept so soundly?[7] Who is the thief? God? What a curious way to characterize God; God is the thief who breaks in, rips off everything you've got, purloins all your defenses, and absconds into the night.

That's not a very nice thing to say about God.

Prayer? A desperate widow pleads her case before a scoundrel of a judge.[8] But she gets nowhere. So she shows up at his residence in the middle of the night and begins beating on his front door, screaming at the top of her lungs, "Help me! Give me justice!"

The judge says to himself, "Though I don't give a rip about these old women and their plight (justice means nothing to me), in order to get this old bat out of my hair, I will get up and give her what she demands." Pray like that, says Jesus. Like what?

These parables are like windows through which we see into the heart of God. Yet sometimes, when you gaze through a window, there is a moment when you catch the reflection of your face. The glass in the windowpane becomes a mirror. You see yourself. Parables can be like that.

With whom did you identify in the opening parable of the dishonest manager? At first, your sympathy is with the poor little manager. Sure, stealing is not a virtue, but who sympathizes with the rich? The manager is probably getting back only what the boss should have paid him in the first place.

But when the swindle begins, when we learn what a lazy loser this manager really is, we find ourselves up in the front office with the boss saying, "I don't see how you put up with that little crook all these years. Are you aware that he's hustling you out of a fortune? Hang him!"

But then, when the judgment comes and the dishonest manager stands before the boss, you are aghast when the boss praises the little sleaze as a business genius. This was the disreputable boss with whom you identified? It makes me wonder about your ethics.

So here we are, rushing to and fro in this story, desperately trying to find the one good person—that is, the person who is like us— the character with whom we can identify. Yet, in the end, we're frustrated by the realization that they are all crooks. Everybody, high and low, rich and poor, is a sleaze. Nobody's hands are clean, including yours.

What sort of teacher would tell a sleazy little story like this to people like us?

You and I tell stories in order to figure out what sort of world we've got. Stories are fiction that is meant to uncover the deep, real truth about the world. Nobody can live without a story that makes sense of the world and gives us a beginning, a middle, and an end to what could otherwise be a really random world.

And yet, Jesus' parables tend not to explain. They just begin, as if out of nowhere, without context, often in the middle. They are, at times, exasperatingly devoid of important details. As we have noted, few of the parables have well-wrought conclusions. They seem more intent on confusion than clarification. Surely, Jesus could have found a more effective mode of explaining his message—unless explaining of his message was not his chief goal.

Jesus' first hearers share our frustration. "Why do you talk in parables?" his disciples asked.[9] Why, Jesus? Matthew remembers Jesus replying: "To you has

Aside to Jesus: Some people buy books like this one hoping that the book will explain you, make the complicated simple and the mysterious comprehensible, and thereby make you easier to swallow without choking. I guess you aren't going to let us get away with that, are you?

been given the gift to understand the great secrets of the kingdom of heaven, even though few of you are the brightest candles in the box. But to the rest of them everything's a riddle. I tell these stories so they can hear things they wouldn't otherwise hear."[10]

First insight: understanding of Jesus, faith in Jesus, the ability to figure out what he's talking about and what he's up to, is a gift of God. It's God's revelation, not some personal intellectual achievement,

"I throw out so many of these parables because, listening, they don't hear and, looking, they don't see," says Jesus.

Second insight: mere understanding of Jesus may not be the point. Parables take you deeper. They are a complex, deep way of thinking about the world. It is possible to think too quickly or superficially that you know Jesus. Then, you can pigeonhole Jesus and forget about him, thinking about Jesus in about the same way you think about everything else. You walk away murmuring, "I got it." Maybe the parables want to expose you to the adventure that comes with, "Jesus got me." Maybe Jesus tells these stories in order to make you a character in the story, in order to put your life in the grand narrative of God's salvation of the world.

By the way, just in case you are too pleased with Matthew's explanation of Jesus' penchant for parables, Mark remembers Jesus saying, "Why do I speak in parables? I talk like this so that they won't hear no matter how closely they listen and they won't see no matter how sincerely they look."[11] Why on earth would the church include two passages, from the mouth of Jesus, contradicting one another? It's a riddle.

Are you willing to follow a Savior who deals in incomprehensible riddles and crazy jokes?

Third insight: eventually, this sometimes contradictory, conflicted quality of Scripture, which often is so exasperating may, with time, become beloved. Sometimes, Jesus reaches out for us; sometimes, Jesus pushes away. Jesus is God with us, not God controlled, explained, and tamed by us. Jesus not only spoke in parables; Jesus *is* a parable.

There was a time when people thought that Jesus told lots of these stories because he was attempting to put difficult ideas into simple, everyday rural idiom. You can readily see that explanation doesn't do justice to the complex, disarming, disorienting quality of most of these parables. Their surprise endings, or lack of endings, their cryptic, enigmatic quality, the way they delight in making heroes out of scalawags and Samaritans suggest that parables are meant to dislodge more than to explain.

Why, Jesus? Why do you talk in riddles? Story by story, Jesus is moving us from the safe, secure world we thought we knew to another world where all is strange and things don't turn out as expected, and something's afoot. You are forced to review your inherited assessment of the world. You are disconnected from your old, familiar world so that, now, you might be connected to a whole new world. God turns out to be other than you previously had assumed. The kingdom of God dawns in that moment when, from the ditch, you look down the Jericho Road, having lost your last, best hope of rescue by a nice savior, only to see coming toward you the lousy Samaritan you despise.

Some of Jesus' other great hits: The kingdom of God is like a mustard seed, smallest seed in all the world—Jesus was prone toward hyperbole— which, when planted, germinates, grows, and becomes a tree. Birds can rest on its branches.[12] Actually, the mustard plant is a nuisance weed (not much of a "tree") that might grow to a height of two or three feet. I can hear the disciples protesting, "Jesus, we don't like you referring to us as a weed." Then, I hear Jesus respond to his uniquely unimpressive disciples, "Be glad that what is unimpressive to the world impresses me."

The kingdom of God is like a man who, plowing a plot of rented land, uncovers buried treasure.[13] He rushes to the owner of the property and, feigning casual interest, asks, "How much would you take for that worthless piece of rock-ridden dirt?" The kingdom demands extreme action; it is not for the squeamish of heart or for those who are too ethically constrained.

Only the storyteller who delighted in telling us the story of the thieving employee and the thief-commending boss would delight in a tale about dishonest real estate dealings, calling it all "the kingdom of God."

The kingdom of God is like a man who calls in his slaves and dumps his entire holdings on them, without a word of instruction or care, and then leaves town. This kingdom begins in a reckless gamble.[14]

"Thy kingdom come," Jesus taught his disciples to pray.[15] How does it come? What are we to do? The kingdom of God is like a man who scattered seed on the earth then went home and went to sleep. While he slept, the seed germinated, a stalk, then the kernels of grain appeared, miraculous harvest.[16] Sorry, all you conscientious, spiritually high-achieving religious eager beavers. God's realm is something God does. A gift. Grace.

> Aside to Jesus: To all of us spiritual eager beavers and God go-getters, it's a jolt to hear that the kingdom of God is something *you* do, rather than something *we* do.

God's realm is at once so very strange—like a thief in the night, seed growing secretly, undeserved miraculous harvest, treasure in a field—and at the same time, so very close, ordinary, and real—like seed, weeds, fish, and shady business deals. The kingdom is that realm ruled by the God who manages to be at once so close to us and also quite far from us, a God we could never have thought up without outrageous parables. The truth about God is a truth that is comprehended only parabolically. Jesus almost never sounds like us preachers—full of principles, platitudes, pronouncements, three-point sermons, eternal, absolute, unarguable assertions. Jesus' truth is concrete, close to the stuff of daily life, yet enigmatic, beyond daily life, ambiguous, open to debate, demanding rumination and interpretation.

That dark night when Jesus was arrested, the disciples, in an attempt to save their own skins, flee into the darkness. Mark says that a "young man" who was with them is grabbed by one of the soldiers, and he too flees into the darkness, naked, leaving a surprised soldier holding nothing but the youth's robe.[17]

Who is that naked man? What was he up to? Why would Mark mention him here, at this climactic moment in the story of Jesus? Early commentators speculated that the young man was one of the unnamed disciples. Some said he was a prefigurement of Jesus—just as Jesus shortly will give death the slip, leaving his shroud in the tomb, so the young man has given death the slip—an advance sign of the coming resurrection. Truth is, nobody has any idea why he was there.

I love these unexplained, unusable events in the story that remind us that we may come to know and love Jesus, but we will never, ever control, grasp, or hold on to Jesus anymore than the soldiers capture that young streaker.

I've spent my whole adult life studying the parabolic teachings of Jesus. And yet I confess that, to this day, I really don't know for sure why Jesus told the parable of the dishonest manager who swindled his boss and who, in turn, was goofily praised by his boss. I don't know what to do with such a patently absurd story. Why, Jesus?

Perhaps I'm not to do anything with the story or the rabbi who dared to tell it to a nice, cautious, rational person like me. Maybe, in telling this story, the rabbi is trying to do something with me.

What is God like? A man had two sons.[18] (It is known by us as "The Prodigal Son," although Jesus doesn't give his parables titles.) The younger son says, "Father, give me my inheritance." In other words, drop dead. (Is there any other way to put the old man's will into effect?) And the father does just that. Here we see an image of maturation which is most congenial to our society. America was built by immigrants, people who left their parents to seek their fortunes in this "far country" of a New World. And they, in turn, taught their children that the only way to get anywhere was to immigrate, to leave home, and to sever parental ties.

Out in the "far country," Jesus says the boy engages in "loose living." Pause just a moment to allow your imagination to work with that phrase, "loose living." Though Jesus doesn't, feel free to supply whatever forms of "loose living" appeal to you—loose girls, loose boys, chocolate cake.

With all the money wasted on loose living, the young man is reduced to the level of a pig. Imagine him in rags, swilling the pig slop to his porcine comrades. Eventually, it was hangover, empty pockets, wake-up time, Monday morning. The boy "comes to himself." He says, "Wait a minute. I don't have to starve out here. I have a father, a home."

And he turns back toward home. He has written a little speech for the occasion. "Now look, Dad. Before you start yelling, let me explain why she answered the phone when you called my room," or "Dad, er, uh, I mean,

32

Father, I have sinned. I am unworthy to be called your son. Treat me as one of your hired servants."

But the father isn't interested in speeches.

"Chill, Howard," says the father. "Save the flowery speeches for your application to law school. Come on in. I'll show you a real party."[19]

Which is why this story has always been a shocker. We thought Jesus came to jack up ethical standards, to put a bit more muscle into our moral fiber. Here is the homecoming of a ne'er-do-well as a party. It isn't what we expect. We want the father to be gracious, but not overly so. Homecomings for prodigals are fine, when prodigals are dressed in sackcloth and ashes, not in patent leather pumps and a tux. Our question is the same as that of the older brother, "Is it fitting to throw a party for a prodigal?"

It's a parable about a party thrown by a father for a prodigal. Jesus, in telling this story, expends more verses describing the party than on any other aspect in the story.

Put this parable in context. One day, Jesus' critics cried, "This man eats and drinks (that is, parties) with sinners! What kind of Savior are you?"[20]

You expect Jesus to back off, saying, "I'm going to redeem these whores and tax collectors! Make 'em straighten up, be more responsible and middle class, like you and me."

No. He tells them that God loves to party with sinners, tells them parables of a party when a woman found a lost coin, and a bash after a shepherd found a lost sheep, followed by the biggest, most questionable blow-out of all—the party for the prodigal son. So, "they began to make merry." In the return of the wayward son from the "far country," Jesus dramatizes a return from exile. Israel's long deportation is ending. Come home, and join the great kingdom party! End of Scene One.

Scene Two: Now the music shifts from James Brown to Buxtehude, and in comes, in grand procession, the Dean of Students, Trustee Committee on Student Behavior, and Chair of the Judicial Board, all escorting their favorite character in the story—the older brother.

Nostrils flared, looks of indignation: "Music! Dancing! Levity! And on a Wednesday! What are you doing in that tux?" the older brother asks the servant.

"Your kid brother's home. The old man has given everybody the night off, and there's a party."

"A party! Doesn't that old fool know that we've got turnips to dig? How does he expect me to keep down overhead when he goes and wastes two grand on a party to welcome home this son of his who blew his hard-earned money on whores?"

Wait a second. When Jesus was telling the story earlier, did he say anything about whores? All he said was that the younger son blew his money in the far country on "loose living." Perhaps all that means is that he slept in late and ate high-cholesterol snacks.

But see? The converse of the older brother's, "See what a good boy am I," is always, "See what this son of yours has done . . . harlots, whores!"

The older son was angry and wouldn't go in. The father comes out into the darkness and begs him to come to the party.

"Lo, these many years have I served you," the older son sneers to the old man, "turning your turnip business around, putting the books in the black."

"Come on in, Ernest," says the father. "So what? You're the biggest turnip grower in Des Moines. Big deal. At least your kid brother has been to the city and tasted the wine. Come on in. Let's party."

Aside to Jesus: A high percentage of those of us who would plunk down money for a book about Jesus are responsible, stay-at-home older brothers or sisters who don't appreciate your being so tough on the older sibling in this story, I fear. You don't make it easy for us, do you, Jesus?

As it turns out, the most interesting character in the story is not the prodigal son or the older brother. It's the father. He's the real prodigal because his love is extravagant, more excessive than either the younger brother's loose living or the older brother's moral rectitude. It's a story about a parent who is excessive in his persistence to have a family, an old man who meets us when we drag in from the far country after good times go bad and who comes out to the lonely dark of our righteousness and begs us to come in and party. It's a hopeful, joyous story of homecoming; it's a somber warning to those who would rather sulk in the dark than come in and join the homecoming dance.

"You are always with me. Everything I've got is yours," pleads the father out in the dark with the older brother. The father is willing to miss the first dance in the hope that his firstborn might relent his vaunted self-righteousness and join the party.

The Bible never questions: "Is there a God?" The Bible's question is: "Who is the God who is there?" John says that nobody has ever seen God until we met the one who told this parable.[21] God is the long-suffering parent who waits for the younger son to come home when good times go bad and who also pleads with the older boy to come in, hug his brother, resume the family, and "make merry." The story's claim that God is the parent who refuses to stop silently waiting or earnestly pleading for you collides with modern self-understanding that our lives are our possessions, like a Chevrolet, to do with as we please. We are owned, the story implies, sought, even loved. The story also collides with the modern view of God as a detached, rule-driven, distant potentate who can't stand for the kids to have a good time.

Jesus' story doesn't have an ending. We are not told if the younger brother ever grew up and bought a Buick or if the older brother ever loosened up and joined the party. We doubt that they "lived happily ever after." (I told you this was a true story.) Jesus doesn't end the story, because this is the kind of story which you finish yourself. And you do, even if you don't know it. I'm betting that the one whom the father is awaiting, the one whom he is begging to come in and party, is you. This story says: you journey not alone. There is One who names you, claims you, has plans for you, waits or prods, invites, or blesses you. This One, sooner or later, will have you.

Jesus not only could recite this psalm by heart, he enacted it in his stories and life: "O LORD, you have searched me, and known me. / You know when I sit down and when I rise up; . . . / You search out my path and my lying down, . . . / You hem me in, behind and before, / and lay your hand upon me. . . . / Where can I go from your spirit? / Or where can I flee from your presence?"[22]

We have been found.

YOU CAN LOOK IT UP

1. *pilfering from him.* Luke 16:1 ff.
2. *this story.)* Luke 16:1-12.
3. *in a ditch?* Luke 10:25-37.
4. *wasn't a parable.* Mark 4:34.
5. *into the sea.* Matthew 13:47 ff.
6. *inept fig tree.* Luke 13:6-9.
7. *slept so soundly?* Luke 12:39.
8. *of a judge.* Luke 18:3 ff.
9. *disciples asked.* Matthew 13:10.
10. *"otherwise hear."* Matthew 13:13-16.
11. *"sincerely they look."* Mark 4:11-12.
12. *on its branches.* Luke 13:19f.
13. *uncovers buried treasure.* Matthew 13:44 ff.
14. *a reckless gamble.* Matthew 25:15 ff.
15. *to pray.* Luke 11:1 ff.
16. *miraculous harvest.* Matthew 13:18 ff.
17. *the youth's robe.* Mark 14:51-52.
18. *had two sons.* Luke 15:11-32.
19. *"a real party."* Thanks to Robert F. Capon, in his book *The Parables of Grace*, Eerdmanns, 1988, pp. 129-144, for this fun way of retelling this parable from Luke 15.
20. *"Savior are you?"* Matthew 24:49; Luke 15:2.
21. *told this parable.* John 1:8.
22. *"from your presence?"* Psalm 139:1-7.

CHAPTER FOUR

PARTY PERSON

G od is not a human being"[1] is an undisputed, consistent, scriptural tru-
ism—until we met Jesus.

Many people who first met vagabond, troublemaker, storyteller Jesus
knew he was a person of a very special sort. As a Jewish man, he said and did
things that most human beings do. But he also said and did things—forgiving sins, performing miraculous signs and wonders, speaking for God with
authority—nobody but God can do. Jesus appeared to be so godlike, so at
one with God, that he not only spoke in an easy and intimate way of God as
"Father," but quite early on, his followers spoke of him as "Son of God."
Particularly after his resurrection, his divinity seemed self-evident to those
who worshiped him and experienced his presence. He embodied and
demonstrated as much of God as we hope to see. Yet even in his resurrection, even in his freedom from many of the binding limitations upon us,
Jesus still had a kind of body, still ate breakfast with his disciples on the
beach, still broke bread with them at suppertime.

Nobody doubted that Jesus had a body. He spit in the dirt.[2] He bled and
hurt like hell on the cross. After a full day on the road, he was tired.[3] He
got angry, especially with people who presumed they were tight with God.[4]
On a couple of occasions, he broke down and wept.[5] In every way, except
sin, Jesus fully shared our humanity. The gospels depict him not as some
disembodied spirit fluttering above human life. In order to do something
about the human problem, Jesus had to become human. As the Letter to the
Hebrews puts it, if Jesus was God with us, God doing something decisive
about the problem of us, then "he had to become like his brothers and sisters in every respect."[6]

Though Jesus was a male, his gender seems almost irrelevant to him or to
his message. Jesus once compared himself to a mother hen who gathers her
chicks under her wings.[7] Although Jesus lived in a patriarchal culture, Jesus

37

never said anything demeaning about women and even praised some women as being more perceptive than his male disciples; he appeared to have considered some of these women to be among his inner circle. Paul once said that it was terrible for women to "speak in church," but Jesus had no problem whatsoever with women speaking to him. In casting himself in the role of a servant, the role that most cultures have imposed upon women, Jesus pioneered—for both men and women—a different image of what it means to be human. Jesus redefined both "humanity" and "divinity," so people never again could think "human being" or "God" without thinking of Jesus. The church eventually expended much effort to guard the mystery of the co-mingling of humanity and divinity in Jesus. The Scriptures offer no explanation of Jesus' divinity and humanity. Rather the Scriptures testify to what everyone who followed Jesus eventually knew: Jesus Christ was fully God *and* fully human. God was "in Christ."[8] To see Jesus is to see the Father of Jesus.[9]

Sorry if you prefer your God to be with you as a remarkably effective moral teacher or wise sage. In Jesus, humanity and divinity meet. A domesticated Jesus, whose strange, inexplicable mix of humanity and divinity has somehow been made simpler—either human or divine, one or the other, and hence easier for us to understand and to handle—is no Jesus at all. Intellectual humility is required, a willingness to let God be complicatedly incarnate, close to us, rather than the simpler God we thought up on our own. Sometimes the strange, rational impossibility just happens to be true—God was in Christ, reconciling the world to himself.

Sorry if you prefer your God to come at you in an exclusively spiritual, inflated, pale blue and fuzzy vagueness, hermetically sealed from where you actually live. In Jesus, divinity and humanity embrace.

Sometimes people ask, "Can I really trust the Bible, seeing that it is a thoroughly human product, full of all the errors and contradictions that characterize any human endeavor?" The implication is that if Scripture has any human taint, shows any creaturely weakness, the Bible can't be trusted to talk about God. But what if Jesus is true? What if we don't know anything for sure about God, except that which is shown to us by the God-and-human Jesus? What if Jesus really is fully human and fully divine? Then where on earth would we expect to know anything about God, except through a medium that is human? God came to us as we are, met us where we live, in the human words of Scripture that become the very voice of God, in the man Jesus who becomes the very presence of God.

Nowhere is Jesus' human nearness (and, in a curious way, his divine distance) more apparent than in the portrayal of Jesus as moving from one dinner party to the next. He was no ragged renunciator of this world. He was a party person. He was never a priest bathed in incense up at the temple; he was a wandering rabbi who did some of his best teaching amid the festivity of the dinner table. Jesus was accused more than once of

> Aside to Jesus: I can't tell you how long it's been since someone, after visiting my church at worship, left saying, "When they're with Jesus, they drink too much, overeat, have too many low-class types among them—and have too much fun."

showing the unseemly behavior of "a glutton and a drunkard, a friend of tax collectors and sinners."[10]

There were times when Jesus went alone into the desert to pray, but we know next to nothing about what actually transpired in that solitude. More typical is for Jesus to be constantly interacting with people—mixing it up with a crowd, meeting travelers on the road, and most typical of all, eating and drinking with gusto at parties. In a world where women were relegated to the home, Jesus welcomed them to travel with him on the road from Galilee to Jerusalem and was entertained by them in their homes. He seemed intent on making the private go public. He loved the give-and-take of public debate.

As a supremely social, communal person, whatever it was that Jesus felt called by his heavenly Father to do, he had no interest in doing it by himself. His life implies that we are fully human, not in our solitude or loneliness but only through a web of relationships and connections with others, including God. Today, Christian worship is generally known not for the opportunities it offers for hushed serenity but rather for its very noisy communitarian conviviality. The chief Christian liturgical act (the Eucharist or Lord's Supper) occurs at a dinner table. Jesus' own gregarious life made oxymoronic the term "solitary Christian." You can't do this faith solo.

When asked to cite the single most important of the commandments, Jesus flatly refused and instead offered a two-fold command to love God with everything we've got *and* to love "your neighbor as yourself,"[11] as if one made no sense bereft of the other.

Whining critics complained, "The disciples of John the Baptist fast often and go about with long faces," (we can tell they're religious; they look so miserable) "but your disciples are always at parties, and eating and drinking."[12] Jesus retorted, "When the groom shows up, do the wedding guests look sad? It's party time!" It's hard to imagine a similar complaint against Jesus' contemporary disciples.

God in Jesus Christ is encountered not through solitary walks in the woods, or even by reading a book (!), but rather at a mundane dinner table, doing that most utterly carnal of acts—sharing food and drink with friends. Jesus really was God incarnate—God localized, humane, and available in the flesh. Thus, Jesus opened his Sermon on the Mount with, "Blessed are those who hunger and thirst for righteousness, for they shall be filled."[13] Nobody goes away hungry from a banquet. Presumably, Jesus' message has more traction among the hungry and thirsty than among the fat and happy. If you are filled, pleased with current arrangements, there's little Jesus can do for you. Don't you find it fascinating that Jesus pitched his message more to those who could say, "I want more. I'm still hungry," than to those who said, "No thanks, I'm full"?

A Pharisee invited Jesus to a soirée.[14] No sooner has grace been said and the wine is poured than a notorious "woman of the city" (make of that what you will) shows up and makes a scene, caressing the feet of Jesus, letting down her hair (yes, that expression meant the same then as now), wiping Jesus' feet with her hair, and, in general, putting the whole party in an uproar.

"If this guy were a real prophet, he could see what a low, sinful sort of woman this is," the Pharisee mutters in a voice loud enough to be heard by everyone at the table. After all, who is a prophet, other than someone who knows a real sinner when he sees one?

Jesus replies to the Pharisee, "Simon, do you see this woman? I show up here expecting a good time, and you didn't kiss me or give me a foot massage. She knows how to get down and party."

Jesus then puts it in a parable: "A man was owed ten dollars by one debtor, ten thousand dollars by another. He forgave both debtors. Now, think hard, Mr. Religious Expert—which man was the most grateful?"

"Er, uh, I guess the one who was forgiven more," answers the Pharisee.

"Do you see this woman as I see her? Her sins, which are great, have been forgiven, so her great gratitude is a bit extravagant," says Jesus. It was not just that Jesus went to parties; it was that he "ate and drank with *sinners.*"

A word in defense of Pharisees: these Pharisees, who always seem to be snipping at Jesus, were the good, pious, holy, biblically knowledgeable religious leaders of Jesus' day. They are not to be interpreted as "Jews" who were opposed to the Jew Jesus. The gospel writers make Pharisees a foil for Jesus, representatives for many of his critics. The Pharisees stand for all of *us* good, true believers who—in our self-righteousness, our presumptive piety and smugness, our great good deeds—infuriate Jesus by our division of the sinners and the saved and our stuff-shirted unwillingness to get down and party.

Though it pains me to admit it, in many of his parables and off-the-cuff comments, Jesus loved to contrast the innocent virtues of "sinners" with the virtues-become-vices of the Pharisees. Many a Pharisee invited Jesus to dinner, only to regret the invitation the minute Jesus went on the attack during the dinnertime conversation.

A warning: Jesus can have the same effect on you if you invite him to dine at your table or if you accept an evening at his. He is an uncomfortable guest and an even more abrasive host. I say that as a religious official who knows lots of Scripture. The Pharisee is me.

These Pharisees were certainly gluttons for punishment; they kept inviting Jesus back to dinner, despite his manners. On another Sabbath evening, Jesus is at a Pharisee's house.[15] Once again, after the opening blessing—for Jews every meal is a religious occasion after the blessing—Jesus notices an unfortunately afflicted man.

"Quiz time, you Bible scholars," mocks Jesus. "I know it's wrong to work on the Sabbath. But is it kosher to do good work on the Sabbath? If you had an ox in the ditch, wouldn't you rescue him? Then why not heal this guy?"

The Pharisees stare in silence at their food.

Noting how some of his fellow guests jockeyed for best seats at the table, Jesus went after the guests with some curious etiquette. "Don't push your way up to the best seats at the head table. Take the lower seats, lest you be embarrassed when a more imminent person than you arrives and you must move down." Widespread surprise around the table. What's the point of a party if not to demarcate your social status at the top of the heap?

Watching the host's delight at Jesus' reprimand of the guests, Jesus turns on him: "As for you, when you give a party, don't invite your stuffed-shirt friends and cronies who can repay your invitation. Invite those who really appreciate a free meal and a night on the town: the poor, the maimed, the blind, and the lame." Widespread confusion around the table. What's the point of inviting to a party some loser who can never invite you to his party in return?

Some sweet pious person blurts out, "Blessed be the person who'll eat bread in the kingdom of God!" It's a reference to the hoped-for great banquet. Messiah will come and set a table where all the poor will be able to eat their fill without having to pay.

"Do you really want to eat at that table?" As usual, this reminds Jesus of a story: "Once upon a time, a man gave a great banquet. He invited his best friends. Astonishingly, they all began to make excuses for their absence: one had just gotten married, another had bought a piece of land and hadn't seen it. (A Near Eastern first-century male lets a new wife keep him from a party? In a part of the world where arable land is at a premium, the other guy has bought real estate sight unseen?) The lord of the banquet, having been so insulted by his friends, goes ballistic and—having already paid the caterers—sends out servants to bring in to the banquet "the poor, and maimed, and blind, and lame." In short, the weird guest list Jesus commended earlier.[16]

There you have it. The kingdom of heaven is a party with a bunch of losers whom you wouldn't be caught dead with on a Saturday night, God's idea of a great time. Revelation says our destiny is one day to party with Jesus forever, to sit down with him at "the marriage supper of the Lamb."[17] Think of the church as a warm-up, front-loading for a party with a bunch of losers that no respectable person would be caught dead with on a Sunday morning.

The prophet Isaiah had foretold a day when all the outcasts and poor of the world would be invited to eat their fill of wine, milk, and honey without paying a dime.[18] All the peoples of the world would be at an eternal victory dinner. In his eating and drinking, partying, and outrageous table etiquette, Jesus portrays that promised party. Trouble is, he is celebrating the coming of God's kingdom with all the "wrong" people.

We dress up and engage in revelry because parties offer a respite from the dull, humdrum world where we live Monday through Friday. But in his partying, Jesus rejects a temporary respite from this world; he shows them a glimpse of this world healed, finished, redeemed, and restored to what God originally intended. At these parties and in his open-handed invitation to all to come join in the fun, it's like Jesus is giving the world a foretaste of the messianic banquet yet to be. This is what reality will be—not just on Saturday night but for all eternity, not just for a fortunate few but for everybody—once God gets God's way and the promised kingdom comes. Jesus is celebrating a great Passover party on the eve of Israel's move from slavery to freedom. He is throwing a victory party, sometime before the final battle, so confident is he about who the victor shall be. He is having a state dinner with a very different guest list. He is the joyful woman throwing a bash for the whole neighborhood now that she has found her lost coin.[19] He is making an in-your-face political statement by inviting those whom the world excludes, to show what the world's defeat looks like when, at last, God's kingdom comes. God's will is done on earth as it always is done in heaven.

The church on Sunday morning is meant to be the party before the party, the bash that lasts an hour on Sunday to get us warmed up, so that we're one day fully able to obey Jesus and party with God and neighbor forever. Kingdom of God time is party time.

Thus today, when the bread is broken, when the cup of wine is poured for Holy Communion, the Lord's Supper, the priest often repeats the words of Scripture, "Christ our Passover is sacrificed for us. Let us keep the feast!"[20]

Early one morning, after the death and resurrection of Jesus, his disciples were at work on the beach, doing that which they did before they met Jesus—fishing. A stranger came and said, "Breakfast is ready." Not one of the disciples had to ask, "Who are you?" They all

> Aside to Jesus: Now I understand why I get so few takers when I say to people outside of the church, "Come! Help us pay our church mortgage!" or, "Come! Let us tell you what's wrong with your life!" Over all this boring church talk, I hear you calling, "Come! Anybody want to get down and party?"

knew, when the stranger took bread and gave it to them, along with some fish. It had to be Jesus.[21] It was none other than the one who exclaimed, "I'm the bread of life! Feed on me!" The party isn't over until God says it's over.

Same thing happened in Luke's account of a supper at Emmaus: "They recognized him when he broke the bread."[22] That same miracle happens on most Sundays in most churches. Not only when we eat the bread and drink the wine of the Lord's Supper but also when we look at the ragtag group of losers who show up for the feast, we see Jesus partying with the losers.

Why Jesus? Why were your nights on the town such an outrage? Why was a wonderful person like you tortured to death by the faithful? We look at the faces around the Lord's table on Sunday, and they are looking back at us, no doubt, knowing our multiple foibles and desecrations. It's then and there that we can well believe that Jesus was murdered because of his behavior at parties. Jesus was crucified for the company he kept. Still is.

YOU CAN LOOK IT UP

1. *"a human being,"* Numbers 23:19.
2. *spit in the dirt.* John 9:6.
3. *he was tired.* John 4:6.
4. *tight with God.* Matthew 23:13.
5. *broke down and wept.* Luke 19:41; John 11:35.
6. *"in every respect."* Hebrews 2:17.
7. *under her wings.* Matthew 23:37.
8. *"in Christ."* 2 Corinthians 5:19.
9. *Father of Jesus.* John 14:9.
10. *"and sinners."* Matthew 11:19.
11. *"as yourself."* Mark 12:30-31.
12. *"eating and drinking."* Luke 5:33.
13. *"they shall be filled."* Matthew 5:6.
14. *to a soirée.* Luke 7:36 ff.
15. *a Pharisee's house.* Luke 14:1 ff.
16. *commended earlier.* Luke 14:15 ff.
17. *"of the Lamb."* Revelation 19:9.
18. *paying a dime.* Isaiah 55:1-13.
19. *lost coin.* Luke 15:8-10.
20. *"keep the feast!"* 1 Corinthians 5:7.
21. *had to be Jesus.* John 21:12-13.
22. *"broke the bread."* Luke 24:35.

CHAPTER FIVE

PREACHER

In the beginning was the Word, and the Word was with God, and the Word was God.
He was in the beginning with God. All things came into being through him,
and without him not one thing came into being.[1]

Thus begins John's Gospel. In this majestic, poetic prelude, we hear an echo of an earlier text, the beginning of Creation: "In the beginning when God created the heavens and the earth, . . . God said. . . . 'Let there be light'; and there was light."[2] There are gods who create by having sex with other gods, or through a primal, cosmic battle between good and evil, chaos and order. But this God creates through nothing but a word. All this God has to do is say, "Light!" and there it is. "Animals!" and where, before, there was nothing but formless void, there is now something—giraffes, hippos, aardvarks, all sprang from the word.

On a cloudless night, this God called Abram, a nomadic desert sheik, out of his tent and promised to make a great nation from this childless old man and his aged wife, Sarah. Though the world considered the old couple "barren," God promised Abram that his descendents would be as numerous as the stars and would comprise a nation that would be a "blessing to all the nations."[3] And all this would be on the basis of nothing more than a promise, nothing more than words. That's the way this God gets what he wants: words.

When that promised people did become numerous, they found themselves as slaves in Egypt, under the heel of the most powerful empire in the world. Moses was out in Midian, watching over his father-in-law's sheep. (Moses had killed a man back in Egypt and was on the lam.) Before an astounded Moses, a bush burst into flame, but was not consumed. Even more dumbfounding, the bush talked![4]

"I am the Lord your God. I have heard the cry of my people and have come down to deliver them. Now you go to the Pharaoh and say, let my people go!"

Is that all? God is going to free the Hebrews on the basis of nothing but a command from a none-too-rhetorically-talented and untrained speaker like the murderer Moses?

"Who am I that I should go to the Pharaoh and say . . . ?" asked Moses, who knew his limitations with language.

"Go!" said the Lord. And Moses obeyed, spoke up for the slaves, told the truth to mighty Pharaoh, and led the Children of Israel to freedom. Tradition says that Moses wrote the first five books of the Bible—testimony to what God can do to the linguistically challenged, if we are obedient to God's, "Go!"

That is the way this God works—creating something out of nothing, a people out of nobodies, free women and men out of slaves—all on the basis of nothing but words. What God speaks is.

Those people, who were free under the leadership of Moses, were given a land "flowing with milk and honey," just as God had promised. But they wandered. They talked to other gods, forgot their origins, two-timed the God who had liberated and blessed them. So God sent a peculiar set of preachers called "prophets." These God-obsessed individuals were chosen personally by God to give the people of Israel the bad news of their coming exile, to sustain them through the horrors of their Babylonian captivity, to announce that they were going home, and then to direct how they would reconstruct themselves as God's people—all on the basis of nothing but words. Prophets spoke God's truth to power no matter what the king thought. "Thus says the Lord . . ." began many a prophetic sermon. Violent responses ended many too. The prophets of Israel were poets who were preachers, preachers who were poets. They deconstructed old worlds and envisioned new ones, spoke something out of nothing with some of the most pushy, metaphorical, and powerful speech ever uttered, all with nothing but words.

As one of the psalms tells it, Hebrew religion thought that God could do almost anything by just saying the word. The word of the Lord is a typhoon that causes "oaks to whirl," "strips forests bare," and before whose power the whole earth shouts "Glory!"[5] One reason why I'm writing this book on "Why Jesus?" is that I think I can shake you up, change your life for the better, make you scream "Glory!" and help Jesus get hold of you—with nothing but words.

No sooner does John's Gospel begin with high, mysterious, and poetic echoes of Creation ("In the beginning was the Word . . .") than the word alights to earth, becomes incarnate in Jesus, and gets mixed up in the story of that weird prophet, John the Baptizer. Usually, when God almighty speaks, it is in a human voice, typically the voice of prophets sent by God. By the time of Jesus, many people in Israel figured that the age of prophesy was finished—until Messiah came. Some, when they heard Jesus speak, called him "prophet."[6]

Mark begins with, "Jesus came into Galilee, preaching the gospel of God, shouting a simple sermon, 'The time is fulfilled, and the kingdom of God is at hand; repent, and believe in the gospel.'"[7] What did Jesus do for a living? "He went . . . preaching in their synagogues."[8] Jesus the Christ is God garrulous, loquacious, and graciously talkative.

Luke gives a rather detailed report of Jesus preaching his first (and, I presume, last) sermon at his hometown synagogue in Nazareth. There they handed

> Aside to Jesus: How curious that we are forever complaining that we don't know enough about you, we have too little information about you when, in truth, we have heard more from you than we've ever been able to handle.

him the scroll of the prophet Isaiah. He read the stirring words, "the Spirit of the Lord is upon me to preach good news to the captives." Then Jesus interpreted the Scripture, saying that this prophetic prediction was taking place right then. He recalled two episodes from the work of Elisha and Elijah, great prophets of the past. The congregational response? Murderous rage.

When Jesus the preacher got up in front of the synagogue at Nazareth, he showed the rest of us what speaking a word from God is all about.

First, the preacher speaks under the power of the Holy Spirit. What the preacher says is not just one person's outburst at the moment—it is divinely derived testimony. The preacher speaks under Spirit-induced compulsion. It's not a sermon unless the words of the preacher are empowered by the Holy Spirit and made understandable to the listening congregation through the work of the Holy Spirit. In some mysterious way, God tells the preacher what to say.

By the way, the word for "wind" (*pneuma*) is the same Greek word for "spirit." Genesis says that "a wind from God" brooded over the dark waters and created the world.[9] When Jesus says, "The Holy Spirit is upon me to preach good news," it's as if Jesus is saying that the godly wind that created the world, the dove that descended, and the heavenly voice that spoke at his baptism is the same godly spirit that is empowering him to speak. It's as if a whole new world is being created—Genesis 1 all over again, in his speaking of this word.

Second, the sermon is based upon Scripture ("Scripture" for Jesus was what we call the "Old Testament," or the "Hebrew Scriptures"). The Nazareth congregation didn't ask Jesus to share his feelings with them or to speak from personal experience. They handed him a scroll of the prophet Isaiah and demanded him to work from that. Jesus quotes directly from Isaiah:

> The Spirit of the Lord is upon me,
> because he has anointed me
> to bring good news to the poor.
>
> He has sent me to proclaim release to the captives
> and recovery of sight to the blind,
> to let the oppressed go free,
> to proclaim the year of the Lord's favor.[10]

This ancient written word is presumed to be none other than God's word, here, now.

Third, Jesus clearly believes that these ancient writings provide an accurate clue to what is going on in the present:

"Today, this Scripture is fulfilled in your hearing."

The preacher offers listeners some gospel, that is, "good news" that is more than helpful advice or even truthful statements. Gospel is the good news that is Jesus Christ. In a sense, every time someone faithfully preaches in a church, the church believes it's like that fateful day in Nazareth all over again—Jesus is preaching to his people. As Saint Paul put it, "for we do not preach ourselves, but Jesus Christ as Lord."[11]

In saying, "Today, this Scripture is fulfilled," Jesus' sermon hits home. It's one thing to say that God will move, act, and save one day, someday. It's quite another thing to say God is doing so today, here, "in your hearing." Surely, there was an excited stir among the congregation. At last, God is coming to save, to set things right. And who is more deserving of that divine deliverance than us—with the heel of Rome on our necks, languishing in poverty and oppression? Sure, it took about four hundred years for God to get moving and come for us, but now the preacher has announced our deliverance. Hallelujah!

It was about then that Jesus' sermon went south and the good news got bad.

Jesus said, "No prophet is without honor, except in his hometown." (A nasty little proverb sure to incite the home folks). "Let's see now," said the preacher, thumbing through his floppy, black, leather-bound Bible, "as I recall (quoting from your own Scriptures), there were lots of poor widows right here in Israel during the famine, when prophet Elijah was representing Israel's God, but Elijah fed none of those good Jewish women—only an alien woman of another nation and race."

Sullen silence in the once adoring congregation.

"Again, quoting from our own cherished Scripture, there were surely many sick among us during the days of the great prophet Elisha. The only person healed was this violent, non-Jewish Syrian army officer."

To be reminded by the young preacher that God had come, but had not come as we expected, that God had worked the wrong side of the street before and might well do so again, was quite a blow to the spiritual sensibilities of the good synagogue-going folks at Nazareth.

Aside to Jesus: In all my sermons, I've never had congregational reaction like that. I guess it's because I've found a way to talk about you every Sunday without ever getting hurt for doing it.

Fourth, all hell breaks loose in response to the sermon. When Jesus preaches in the power of the Spirit, directly from Scripture, relating what he says to the congregation's lives, the congregation's response to Jesus' well crafted biblical sermon? They rise up with one accord and attempt to throw him off a cliff. His sermon at Nazareth was not Jesus sharing his feelings or exchanging religious ideas (what preaching sometimes is today). Rather, it was his First Inaugural Presidential Address, an official announcement of the coming Invasion. And in so doing, he really rattled the cages of the faithful.

Jesus not only cites two instances, from Israel's own Scripture, of God showing mercy to outsiders, but he begins his sermon by quoting the prophet who foresaw a day when even foreigners would be welcomed at Israel's temple and be "joyful in my house of prayer . . . for my house shall be called a house of prayer for all peoples."[12] One can imagine how inclusive verses like these, extending the promises of God to outsiders, would go down amid a congregation full of people who bitterly hated their Roman overlords.

Jesus really was a prophet. Whereas prophets Elijah and Elisha sometimes had to stand up to some king and speak truth to power, prophet Jesus had to stand up to a more totalitarian and potentially violent adversary: people like us. I can't figure out how anybody could get the impression that Jesus is some sort of projection of our own wishes and needs; he is a poor servant of our fantasies about ourselves. He loves the truth as much as he loves us, and he tells the truth no matter how bad it stings. "We never heard such as this!" was a typical response to Jesus' sermons. He came not only full of "grace" but also full of "truth," says John.[13] With Jesus, you can't take the grace without being willing to subject yourself to his disruptive truth.

Fifth, Jesus' sermon is about God. In an age when many of us show up at church expecting to hear about us (How can we better our lives? How can I have the courage to get out of bed tomorrow morning?), it's good to be reminded that Jesus spoke in Nazareth primarily about God and only secondarily, and then derivatively, about us. The primary subject of Scripture (Luke 4 or nearly any other) is not us, but God: Who is the God we've got? What's God up to today? Sometimes the intent of Scripture is not to provide answers but rather to provoke questions. The Bible hardly ever begins with us and works toward God. More typical is for the Bible to begin where things began at Nazareth: with God intruding, speaking, causing trouble, and folks staggering out of church saying, "I thought I really knew God until Jesus started preaching."

You can begin to see, after listening to Jesus preach at Nazareth, that while Christians believe that Jesus is more than a prophet, to describe Jesus' preaching as "prophetic" is just right. Prophetic truth-telling, being so rare in our time, is regarded by most people (particularly the powerful and educated) as a form of dementia. I am certain that, if the first century had mood-altering drugs and psychiatry, Jesus would have never made it to the cross; he would have been forced to languish in smiling sedation at a Dead Sea resort.

Today, we're apt to think of a preacher as a person with such an inordinate desire to please, with so highly developed verbal skills that he or she is an expert in saying nothing in such a way that it sounds like a sweet something. So to our ears, Jesus' preaching sounds downright nasty. There was a reason the religious leadership (people in positions like mine) set so solidly against him. Rather than compromise or soften his message in an effort to win them over or sugar-coat his truth with psychobabble ooze to make it easier to swallow, Jesus flung their opposition back in their faces. He charges well-placed religious experts (like me) with extortion and robbery of the people, calls them "evil and adulterous," "faithless and perverse," a "brood of vipers," and "ravenous wolves" (and that list comes from just one of the four Gospels).[14]

We live in a non-judgmental age. "Do not judge," Jesus told his people, "so that you may not be judged."[15] Of course, he said that to his followers, not to himself. At every turn in the road, Jesus was our prophetic judge, even when he wasn't trying to be. His most compassionate works of mercy drew angry rebuke from the religious leaders and exposed the depth of the crowd's ignorance. If it is not for you and me to judge others, it seems to have been open season for Jesus. "Brood of vipers" is not the nicest evaluation of someone, to be sure. Many people thought they were good, Bible-believing folks until Jesus preached to them.

Perhaps we ought to be reminded that no one should presume to play God and pronounce judgment on anyone else's behavior—unless that person happens to be the judge who is also Son of God, our Creator, our Savior, the same "Judge" who said, as he breathed his last, "Father, forgive them. They don't know what they are doing."[16]

Jesus' pronouncements of judgment show him to be a true prophet who loved God's truth more than popular acclaim. He criticized or condemned in order to instigate a dramatic movement of heart, mind, and hands called "repentance." Thus, he not only preached the good news as truth that could be known but also truth that could free,[17] though he knew firsthand that the truth could well make us mad as hell—his sermon in Nazareth being a prime example. He was truth and light, but something in us, John warns, loves the dark and hates the truth.[18]

If Jesus had befriended only the poor and the oppressed, then he would be the darling of all political revolutionaries and romantic lovers of the less fortunate. But the maddening thing was that Jesus also befriended the rich and the oppressor as well, thus pronouncing judgment on the myriad ways we divide up the world between "us" and "them." Jesus lived the maddening message of the one God's inclusive, expansive love—and it was this message that got him kicked out of Nazareth. The messenger became the message. His enactment of divine determination to gather all people, across all boundaries, out-revolutionized the wildest of revolutionaries.

> Aside to Jesus: It's clear that you wanted to reach people, to invite them, to win them to your kingdom. But it's also clear that, even more, you wanted to tell them the truth, even if they turned away. Just why did you love the truth so much, anyway? What did it ever get you, besides a cross?

When his disciples came upon Jesus scandalously fraternizing with a Samaritan woman in broad daylight, John says "they were astonished."[19] Just the sort of reaction one would expect from good, religious people of any age. Though some preachers do, it's hard to imagine any preacher in the lineage of Jesus receiving an invitation to appear on Oprah or to say a few words in the rose garden at the White House.

At one point, Luke joyfully recorded how the Jesus movement was catching on: "Great multitudes accompanied him."[20] Right then, Jesus preached, "Multitudes? I can fix that. If anyone comes to me and does not hate his own father and mother and wife and children and brothers and sisters, yes, even his own life, he can't be my disciple." Though Luke didn't record the response to that sermon, anybody could figure it out. I wonder that Jesus had even twelve who hung around him for his next sermon, don't you?

During another sermon, Jesus casually said, "unless you eat my flesh and drink my blood you are unworthy of me."[21]

"That's hard to hear," said his disciples.

"Will you also go away?" Jesus asked. (After hearing some of Jesus' sermons, some listeners found other things to do on Sunday mornings.)

"Where can we go?" replied his hapless disciples. "You have the words of life." That's the only sensible reason for listening to Jesus. Not that his sermons give your life meaning, or put a lift in your step, or explicate life's dilemmas, but rather because the one who is speaking just happens to be the Son of God, the Savior of the world, Lord of life.

The good news, gospel, was not only the content of Jesus' sermons; it was Jesus. (1) He is the truth. He not only told us the truth about God; he enacted the truth about God. Thus, Jesus set the bar high for evaluating the truth of any preaching purported to be "in Jesus' name." (2) It's not his peculiar truth if it is not followed, obeyed, embodied, and enacted. (3) Jesus would talk to anybody. It's not his truth if it's not true for all.

At Pentecost, when a mob in the street demanded an explanation for the ruckus in the upper room with the descent of the Holy Spirit and the birth of the church, Peter referred to an obscure passage from the prophet Joel:

> I will pour out my spirit on all flesh;
> your sons and your daughters shall prophesy,
> your old men shall dream dreams,
> and your young men shall see visions.[22]

Through most of our history with God, Holy Spirit-induced talk (preaching) was limited to a few charismatic or simply offensive truth-tellers—the prophets. But there will come a day, when Messiah comes, when God's Holy Spirit will be poured out on all. Young upstarts, women and men, maids, janitors, people who never before got to the microphone will speak up and speak out. Everyone will preach truth to power. Everybody, a preacher. That promised age of free speech is now.

Jesus caused an avalanche of free speech in the face of the world's desire to be left alone in silence. That's why Jesus' people tend to be big talkers. They'll go anywhere for the privilege of talking to anybody. And they won't shut up, no matter what the government says. Jesus not only preached but also sent out his disciples to preach to all the villages of Galilee.[23] The Christian faith is an auditory phenomenon. Saint Paul said that all faith "comes from what is heard."[24] So when we gather to worship

Jesus, there is some silence, but not much as we talk, shout, sing, and read about Jesus.

What is God's kingdom like? A sower went forth to sow.[25] Did he carefully plan, diligently preparing the soil for the seed? Hey, it's the kingdom of God! He slung seed everywhere, wasting lots of good seed with reckless abandon.

Of course, much of the seed is wasted—falling along the road (like I say, it was really messy agriculture), gobbled by birds, choked by weeds. Miraculously, some of the seed, a small minority, germinated, took root, and produced a rich harvest. Miraculous, considering all the seed had going against it. Though this seems to be poor agricultural productivity to me, Jesus found it thrilling.

> Aside to Jesus: I'll admit that most of the words we preachers speak are wasted—the Holy Spirit sometimes enlivens a sermon, and sometimes not. But when the Holy Spirit condescends and enables fresh hearing, then the fireworks! Wish you would do it more often to my words. How about a little help from the Holy Spirit right now with the words on this page?

As a preacher, working for Jesus the preacher, having nothing to arm me and help me fight my battles but words, desperately hoping for a hearing, this may be my favorite parable.

YOU CAN LOOK IT UP

1. *came into being.* John 1:1-3.

2. *"there was light."* Genesis 1:1, 3.

3. *"all the nations."* Genesis 18.

4. *the bush talked!* Exodus 3.

5. *"shouts "Glory!"* Psalm 29.

6. *called him "prophet."* John 4:19; 9:17.

7. *"in the gospel."* Mark 1:14-15 NKJV.

8. *"in their synagogues."* Mark 1:39.

9. *created the world.* Genesis 1:2.

10. *the Lord's favor.* Luke 4:18-19.

11. *"Christ as Lord."* 2 Corinthians 4:5 NIV.

12. *"for all peoples."* Isaiah 56:7.

13. *"truth," says John.* John 1:14.

14. *the four Gospels.* Matthew 7; 12; 17; and 23.

15. *"not be judged."* Matthew 7:1.

16. *"are doing."* Luke 23:34.

17. *that could free,* John 8:32.

18. *the truth.* John 3:19.

19. *"were astonished."* John 4:27.

20. *"accompanied him."* Luke 14:25 ff.

21. *"unworthy of me."* John 6:53, paraphrased.

22. *shall see visions.* Joel 2:28.

23. *villages of Galilee.* Mark 6:6-13; Luke 10:1-12.

24. *"from what is heard."* Romans 10:17.

25. *forth to sow.* Matthew 13:18.

CHAPTER SIX

MAGICIAN

Lazarus, whom you love is ill, come quickly," entreated Jesus' good friends, Mary and Martha, Lazarus' sisters who lived in Bethany.[1] Oddly, Jesus lingered where he was for three more days. What was he doing that was so important? John just says that Jesus hung out where he was for "three more days."

Of course, when Jesus finally shows up in Bethany three days later, it was all over but the weeping; Lazarus had been entombed for three days. Martha gave Jesus a piece of her mind for his malingering. If Jesus loved Lazarus so much, why did it take him so long to get there? He must have loved something else even more.

Upon hearing that Lazarus was dead, John says, "Jesus wept." It's a comfort that Jesus feels our pain, his humanity connecting with ours. Then Jesus said something strange: "I am the resurrection and the life." He didn't say that he has come to tell grieving Martha about the resurrection. He didn't say, "Martha, take heart, one day, someday, your brother will be resurrected, and then you'll get to see him again in heaven." Jesus never talked like that.

Rather, Jesus says, "*I* am the resurrection and the life." Wherever I am, even here at this time and place of death, there is resurrection, and there is life, here, now. With that, Jesus acts on his compassion, goes out to the cemetery and, in a voice loud enough to wake the dead, shouts, "Lazarus, arise!" Lazarus comes forth like a mummy. "Unbind him!" Next thing you know, there's Jesus with Lazarus and his sisters, having a party in Bethany, and Jesus' critics (ever the guardians of the status quo) were planning now to kill him.

Why would you want to kill Jesus for resuscitating a dead man? I'll explain: The authorities had a monopoly on who gets life and who doesn't. They couldn't have some uneducated conjurer running around loose, implying that there's a power available that's as strong as the American Medical Association.

This story is a parable. The church always reads this story on a Sunday in Lent, season of the cross, as a kind of preview of Easter. Even though it's not yet Easter, whenever Jesus, Mr. Resurrection and the Life, shows up at the cemetery, corpses rise, the dead walk, things are cut loose, and the clergy get nervous.

Still, the thing I can't get out of my head is that Jesus refused to rush right over and heal Lazarus, whom he loved. Why, Jesus? Could Jesus have been doing something more important than serving as a member of the health-care delivery team? Though Jesus eventually resuscitated his friend, at some point later, Lazarus died, as all of us must. Even the best health care holds death at bay for only a while. Perhaps those three days were meant by John not only as a prefiguration of Easter but also a critique of some of our health illusions and obsessions. In our culture, it's almost miraculous to find someone who is not jerked around by sickness, someone who doesn't drop all other commitments and responsibilities and allow sickness to dominate his or her life.

> Aside to Jesus: The only time when most church members can expect a call from their pastor is when they are sick. That's curious, in light of the Lazarus story. Sometimes, it takes more courage for a pastor to be with people who are fat, happy, and content than when they are hurting, down, and out.

What does it mean for us to be sick? In Jesus' first-century world, they didn't have our modern systems of immortality management, er, that is, "healthcare system." They had the temple, the priesthood, and Scripture. God said to Adam and Eve, "You are dust and to dust you shall return."[2] Sickness is a prelude to that eventual mortal demise. Then as now, sickness was a sign that this world, for all of its beauty, was also a place of periodic pain, a sign that you were out of whack with the cosmos, a painfully obvious, all-consuming, unwelcome reminder of finitude and vulnerability—your origin and destiny in dirt.

So what did you do when you fell ill? You went to the first-century equivalent of the officially certified, governmentally sanctioned healthcare professional: the priest. He told you what to do with your pain: "Take two doves, have them properly sacrificed at the temple's high altar, and call me in the morning. Follow my prescription and you'll be all fixed up." Like today, this system was fine for those who had the resources to pay for all this expert attention. But what if you were poor (illness and the inability to work usually went hand-in-hand) and couldn't afford the doves, much less a trip to the specialists at the Jerusalem altar?

Too bad for you. You were locked out of the healthcare-immortality system. No life-giving, liberating medicine for you. Your only hope was to contact one of those half-baked wandering magicians who, shunned by all respectable, educated people of means, traveled about taking advantage of the gullibility and desperation of the suffering poor by offering them their magical healing arts for a small fee.

Now, note carefully: Jesus was a magician.

For some time now, at least since the birth of science, Jesus' miraculous work has been an embarrassment for us sophisticated, modern, Western people. We can take Jesus as a teacher, but Jesus as a magician is a turnoff. We believe in medicine, the beneficent side of science, not magic or voodoo, which nobody but crackpots practice.

It might help our thinking about Jesus to clarify the difference between magic and medicine. Whether in first-century Palestine or twenty-first-century America, it's medicine when we believe it works and the government certifies it. It's magic when we affluent, respectable people don't believe in it and only non-credentialed people practice it in the ghetto. All healing, even that of the most expensive, university-related hospitals, is to a great degree faith healing. Our doctors don't just need to be competent, they need to be perfect and potent; they need to look like God.

Our exorbitant faith in and vast expenditures for the medical system may be due more to our income and our social class (and to our idolatry?) than to our scientific superiority to first-century Palestinians. I don't care how well my high-tech surgery goes, there is still a one hundred percent chance that I will die. About the best that medicine can do is to alleviate some of the discomfort of being an animal instead of an angel and briefly to postpone my eventual descent into dust. That Jesus was what we would dismiss as a mere magician says something about him and much about us.

Surely, this is a major reason why Jesus' healing work caused controversy. Even Jesus' most severe critics, who had no intention of following him anywhere, agreed that Jesus performed many signs and wonders.[3] Jesus met a blind man who implored him to restore his sight.[4] Jesus spit in the dust, made a mud paste, put it on the man's eyes, and the man saw. Upon seeing this, the crowd argued over whether or not Jesus had a license to do ophthalmology. If you think it is strange that the crowd didn't celebrate the blind man's healing, then you don't know what a threat

Aside to Jesus: Though healing was clearly not the sole purpose of your ministry, I am struck by how many sick, crippled, insane, and demon-bedeviled people sought you out in your three years of ministry. Far more people at the end of their ropes looked to you for help than have sought me out in my forty years as a pastor. Perhaps I have had a too-limited view of ministry.

this sort of unlicensed, uncontrollable power is to the keepers of the status quo.

So when John the Baptizer sent emissaries to Jesus, asking, "Are you the Messiah, or should we look for somebody else?"[5] Jesus lists some of his wonders as evidence for who he is: the blind, the lame, and the deaf restored to health, the dead raised. Then Jesus says something odd: "and blessed is the one who takes no offense in me." The response of many who witnessed Jesus' miracles was not gratitude or wonderment but offense? Why, Jesus?

With the exception of his friend Lazarus, all of those whom Jesus healed were unknown to him; none of them seemed to have been his followers. The gospels simply mention, from time to time, that Jesus healed, though we know next to nothing about the recipients of his mercy. (No grateful beneficiary of Jesus' healing stepped forth to say a good word in his behalf at his trial and crucifixion.) The emphasis is not on them but rather upon Jesus. There appears to be no formula, no certain path to healing, no set of requirements; magical Jesus healed as a spontaneous, gratuitous outbreak of the kingdom of God. It's a "miracle" precisely because those who were healed had little to do with it.

Note that none of the gospels calls any of Jesus' healing works a "miracle." "Miracle" is our word for inexplicable phenomena that appear to arise from sources other than ourselves. It's always the crowd that is so astonished by Jesus' miraculous moments; never Jesus, as if his wondrous work was the most natural thing in the world. What we label as "miracle," odd, out of this world, an intrusion into the accustomed order of things is what the gospels regard as normal now that Jesus is here. Jesus does these things naturally, giving us a privileged glimpse of the way the world is intended to be. Thus, Jesus challenges our notions of "natural" and "supernatural." "Supernatural" is that weird, prescientific, unverifiable, inexplicable realm to which we relegate everything we don't know how to think

> Aside to Jesus: Why are we so scared of miracles? Is it because, in a do-it-yourself culture, the miraculous is an affront to our presumptions of self-sufficiency? When some people say, "A miracle never happened to me," maybe it has more to do with their lack of imagination than a paucity of your miraculous activity.

about. Maybe what we call "natural" is a perversion of what God intended and what we call "supernatural" is the way the world really is. Maybe the miracles, which to our eyes appear "supernatural," are, to the eyes of God, the most "natural" thing in the world. Though Jesus was accused of turning the world upside down, maybe he was turning the world right side up.

John's Gospel calls the wonders that Jesus periodically preformed "signs." That's the best way to think of Jesus' wondrous work: a sign. A healing, as impressive as it is, is a sign that points to something going on that's even more important. Sometimes in John's Gospel, a miracle is a catalyst for faith,[6] but sometimes all that wonders do is attract people to Jesus who only want to be fed or cured of what ails them and have nothing to do with faith that Jesus is the Christ, the Messiah.[7] Once, after Jesus had fed a multitude, an enthusiastic group wanted to crown him king. Jesus had contempt for their adulation, telling them that they believed in him only because they ate their fill.[8] In other words, they got the "sign" wrong. Following Jesus, being his obedient disciple, required more than a fascination for spiritually strange phenomena. If Jesus' desire, in performing his "signs and wonders," was to make faith in him easier, he failed.

Jesus' healing wonders serve as parables pointing to the truth of who Jesus really is and the direction the world is really headed now that Jesus is on the move. Signs are not proofs; they are pointers, glimpses of who God is and what God wants. (Jesus had some choice words for people who demand proof.)[9]

Of course, signs and wonders don't tell us modern people much, because we like to believe that we live in an orderly, cause-and-effect world governed by natural laws, where miracles are not permitted. In the modern age, we want to control the world around us; because miracles are beyond our control, we exclude them from consideration. Jesus' miracles disrupted the perceived world and indicated that there was more going on with Jesus and with us than we first imagined. Something is afoot.

So John's Gospel presents Jesus as going head-to-head with some of the most popular gods of the classical world, principally through his magical works of power. He turns water into wine[10] (an affront to the god Dionysus, who had the wine monopoly), he miraculously produces bread[11] (Demeter thought she was in charge of grain), and he heals[12] (cutting into the practice of Dr. Asclepius, god of medicine).

As Saint Augustine said, Jesus' miraculous feeding of the multitudes is not much more of a miracle than what happens at the bakery every day. His turning water into wine is not too different from what happens regularly in France and California—if only we had eyes to see that which we relegate to the "natural" is, in the eyes of faith, a sign of a miraculously loving God. Much of what we call miraculous happens all the time in hospitals, just with more time, and with the illusion that the healing that happens there is a commodity that we bought through our healthcare plan.

Jesus knew his magic to be prone to misunderstanding. Much of the healing that occurred in first-century Judea (particularly among the poor) was accomplished by wandering wonder workers. Those whom they healed, while undoubtedly grateful for the healing arts of these miracle-makers, never said, "The one who healed me is the Son of God." Nor did Jesus' miracles provide much reason for believing that Jesus was indeed the Messiah who told the truth about God, particularly for those who expected Messiah to operate within the confines of the official worldview. Hence the almost immediate linkage of questions about authority with his miracles—"Who credentialed this Galilean rabbi to do this?" If anything, Jesus' healing wonders were a hindrance rather than a help to faith, as is shown in the recurrent response, "Who is this?" When one considers our fascination with miracles (see Jesus on a tortilla, and you will get a spot on Fox News), the amazing thing is not that the gospels report Jesus doing many miracles but rather that the gospels report so few. Jesus appears not to want a bunch of miracle-bedazzled gawkers; he wants disciples.

In the earliest accounts of Jesus feeding the multitudes, Jesus was busy teaching a huge crowd out in the wilderness. His intent was to teach. But, as sometimes occurs with professors, he went on a bit long. The day grew late. The sun was setting.

"Master, it's late! End your lecture! The people have nothing to eat!" said the disciples. (Interesting that it takes the disciples to note that the people are hungry.)

Then we get the disciples' answer to human need, "Send them away so they can go back to town and buy themselves some food."

Jesus astonishes his disciples by asking, "What do you have? You give them something to eat."

"Us? All we've got is a few loaves and a couple of cold fish. Where are we to get enough food? There must be five thousand people here," the disciples responded.

Jesus took what his disciples had, blessed it, broke it, and gave it. And wonder of wonders, all "ate their fill."

It's miraculous, for sure. But note the peculiar way that the miracle is almost an interruption in the mission of Jesus (in this case, teaching) and the way in which Jesus utilizes whatever his disciples have among them in order to work his miraculous feeding. He takes what we have, blesses it, and gives it to nourish a hungry world. Can you see why this is the only miracle reported in all four Gospels? It's impressive that Jesus feeds a multitude; it's perhaps more impressive that, sometimes, he uses the modest gifts of ordinary people like us to do miraculous work.

Though Jesus healed many, he didn't heal everybody. He walked by all the sufferers laid out on pallets by the magical pool and unceremoniously healed only one crippled man who had been lying there for years.[13] He was downright annoyed when huge crowds dogged him and interfered with his teaching.[14] As important as health and wholeness were to Jesus, something else was even more significant. He never once told his disciples that, if they loved and obeyed him, he would free them from all pain and misery. Just the opposite; he told them that there would be a cross for every one of them. Rather than be the great palliative for people, Jesus put most of his followers in greater pain than they would have had if he had not called them. Thus, I did a double take when I passed by a church with a sign out front that proclaimed, "A Place of Healing for Hurting People: Come Join Us." I fear it's guilty of false advertizing.

There were some, but not many, who witnessed Jesus' miracles and believed in him. Those of us with good cholesterol numbers and health insurance find belief more difficult, not because we are less credulous than others but because we have overweening faith in the government and its authority to define the world. I fear I would have been among the educated, urbane scoffers who would have sneered, "Who is this who even forgives sins and has this unruly disregard for the inviolate laws of physics?"

Jesus regarded his miracles as ambiguous at best, often charging people to keep quiet about them.[15] When he healed people, he seemed to do it simply as overflowing compassion for those who suffered and as a sign that the kingdom of God was breaking out among them. In other words, when he healed someone, or when he produced an overflow of bread to feed hungry people in the wilderness, it was a sign that God's kingdom had come close, that God's intentions for the world had surged forth.

The gospels themselves display an ambivalent attitude toward Jesus' "wonders and signs." Luke says that when John the Baptizer sent emissaries to Jesus inquiring, "Are you the long-awaited Messiah or should we look for somebody else?" Jesus replied by referring to his wonders, "The blind receive their sight, the lame walk, the lepers are cleansed, the deaf hear, the dead are raised, the poor have good news brought to them."[16] Jesus named the specific, messianic acts that he performed as a validation of his identity. (The preacher in me just has to point out that Jesus lists preaching good news to the poor right up there with raising the dead.)

Jesus sent out the Twelve "to proclaim the kingdom of God and to heal."[17] Even as a healer, Jesus did not work alone. (Thus his church founded the first hospitals.) He declared that all shall be judged on the basis of, "I was sick and you visited me."[18]

Yet many witnessed Jesus' wonders and were completely unconvinced.[19] Jesus repeatedly tells those who were healed to keep it secret, as if Jesus sensed grave danger in people making erroneous inferences from his healing.

Why, Jesus? Why did you perform miracles? As he said, these good works are signs of the kingdom's intrusion into our world and lives. So when he rebukes demons, he's releasing hostages from their captors and reclaiming enemy territory. Every time Jesus intervened and healed someone or provided food and drink for some hungry person, it was as if he vividly demonstrated that *this* is the way the world is supposed to be, *this* is God's intention for Creation, *this* is normal.

Late one night, Jesus' disciples were huddled in a little boat amid a terrifying storm at sea.[20] (Jews generally prefer the good, solid stuff of earth, the promised land, not the dark, foreboding sea.) But where was Jesus? Asleep on a cushion in the boat.

They awake him, crying, "Lord, don't you care that we are perishing?"

Jesus arises, rebukes the wind and waves, and restores calm. Note that there is no attempt to explain why there are storms and why human beings are frail and vulnerable, exposed to dark dangers. Jesus doesn't do much reasoned explanation. Rather, he does salvation. Jesus rises and makes strong, active, and compassionate response. To the wind and the waves, he commands, "Be still!"

Let's admit that, as modern, Western, scientifically-minded people, we are at a keen disadvantage when it comes to thinking about Jesus' "signs and wonders." The people with whom Jesus first worked assumed that reality is open, porous to the periodic interventions and intrusions of the divine. To the open-minded, miracles were not strange intrusions into the otherwise orderly course of the natural world. Perhaps they believed that there was no natural world other than the world that was moment-by-moment sustained and loved by a creative God. Almost none of us share their assumptions.

We value predictability, order, and control more than surprise, mystery, and wonder. We tend to think of our world as closed, rigidly following certain "natural laws," so that the line between "natural" and "supernatural" is obvious and unassailable. The first thing the modern world had to do, in order to give us the illusion that we were gods unto ourselves and in control of everything, was to close off the possibility that God might intervene or intrude into the world. So if you start out with the assumption that miracles don't happen, don't be surprised when you conclude that the miracles of Jesus didn't happen.

But what if, just for the sake of argument, there is no "natural"—that is, no world that somehow functions and is immune from God? What if what we've been led to call "natural" is, in truth, "creation," the result of God's loving, constant, though often subtle and undetected interaction with the world?

Some find the healing miracles of Jesus to be a revealing and comforting help to their faith in Jesus. Others (and perhaps I place myself in this category) see his signs and wonders and think not, "Only God could do something like this," but rather, "I wonder how he did that?" To be honest, whether or not I find the miracles of Jesus revealing and compelling for faith may be related to the expansiveness of my imagination. Many modern people have contented ourselves with a fairly flat and confined worldview.

But what if we're wrong? What if there is more going on in us and in the world than we have been led to believe by the modern worldview? What if the "modern worldview" is a fiction, just another in the long line of futile human attempts to play God? What if Matthew, Mark, and Luke are right—something's afoot that can never be fully contained or described by our human modes of coping with the unknown? In the miracles, it is as if Jesus pulls back the veil that separates the real from the unreal and shows us what's really going on behind the curtain of our limited notions of what's what. In miracles, God reserves God's right to work in ways that disrupt our settled opinions of just what God can and cannot do.

Aside to Jesus: One of the fun things about being a pastor is that I get to hear some really weird stories told by the laity about your miraculous work among them. Question: how come you seem to delight at doing some of your most miraculous work among untrained, uncredentialed laity rather than among us clergy?

Fortunately, whether or not you find the miracles of Jesus to be a catalyst to faith in Jesus, none of the gospels seem interested in making them a substitute for the main thing: Jesus himself. Jesus is more than a member of the healthcare delivery team. Jesus has come for even more than the alleviation of human suffering due to illness. The one miracle, the central sign, and wonder that puts all else about Jesus into proper perspective is his resurrection. I don't see that it makes much difference whether or not you believe Jesus fed five or five thousand people one late afternoon in Judea.[21] But it is very important for you to believe—or at least to have enough intellectual guts to be on your way to believing—that God did something very different, something uniquely revealing, in raising dead Jesus.

"If it is by the Spirit of God that I cast out demons, then the kingdom of God has come to you,"[22] is Jesus' most explicit statement about his miracles. I think we are meant, not to work ourselves upward from the various little miracles that Jesus worked to the great big miracle of the resurrection (if we can get you to believe he turned water into wine, perhaps we can get you to believe that he made life out of death). Rather, we are to work backward from the great big, unexpected miracle that happened on Easter toward everything else that Jesus said and did. For the first disciples, befuddled by Jesus' unexpected but nevertheless undeniable presence with them after Easter, it was as if everything fell into place.

Now we get it, they said after his resurrection. Now we see that your sporadic healing arts were a sign of a much larger project even than your salubrious work among a few hurting people. Now we see that you are determined to have nothing less than the defeat of sin and death and the whole hurting world delivered back into the hands of God.

On Easter evening, when the disciples were walking to the village of Emmaus, they didn't understand a thing the stranger along the road said to them as he opened the scriptures to them.[23] (Funny how sometimes, when Jesus is walking next to you, you don't recognize him. Let that be a lesson to you.) Yet when, in the breaking of the bread, the stranger was revealed as none other than the risen Christ, they said to one another, "Didn't our hearts burn within us when he taught us on the road?"

Something like that happened across the board when, after the resurrection, it was as if the great curtain was pulled back and, in a stunningly revelatory moment, this once ragtag group of occasionally faithful (but usually faithless) disciples were able to say to one another and to the world, "Jesus is the Son of God, the Savior of the world, the Messiah. This is who God really is. This is who we are to be." In that ultimate sign and wonder is the turning point of history, the beginning of humanity's great turn toward God, initiated in God's grand turning toward us.

The clamor for Jesus' healing touch became so overwhelming that Jesus led his disciples out to the desert for a respite. Alas, by the time they get to the desert, it was anything but deserted. The hurting masses followed them out there and were begging for attention. Jesus looked upon them as wandering sheep without a shepherd.[24] So Jesus asked everybody to sit down on the green grass so he could teach.

Green grass? Repeatedly, we have been told that this was a dry desert. What gives?

Israel's long-awaited Messiah is called the Shepherd. Psalm 23 speaks of God as the shepherd who leads the helpless sheep in "green pastures."[25] Isaiah said that, when Messiah comes, creation will be restored, all will be set right, and "the desert shall rejoice and blossom."[26] Even the driest, dead places shall be green gardens.

Get it? Wherever this magical Jesus sets foot—surprise! All miraculously bursts into bloom. Life, abundant life.

YOU CAN LOOK IT UP

1. *who lived in Bethany.* John 11:1–12:19.
2. *"you shall return."* Genesis 3:19.
3. *signs and wonders.* Matthew 12:24-32.
4. *restore his sight.* John 9:6.
5. *"for somebody else?"* Luke 7:20-22, paraphrased.
6. *catalyst for faith.* John 4:53; 11:45-48; 14:11.
7. *the Messiah.* John 6:26.
8. *ate their fill.* John 6:26.
9. *who demand proof.* John 6:26.
10. *water into wine.* John 3:1-10.
11. *produces bread.* John 6:1-15.
12. *and he heals.* John 4:47.
13. *there for years.* John 5:1-9.
14. *with his teaching.* Matthew 4:25.
15. *quiet about them.* Mark 5:43; 7:36.
16. *"brought to them."* Luke 7:20-22.
17. *"and to heal."* Luke 9:2.
18. *"you visited me."* Matthew 25:36.
19. *completely unconvinced.* Mark 3:22, 30.
20. *storm at sea.* Mark 4:35-41.
21. *afternoon in Judea.* Matthew 14:21.
22. *"come to you,"* Matthew 12:28
23. *scriptures to them.* Luke 24:45.
24. *without a shepherd.* Mark 6:34.
25. *in "green pastures."* Psalm 23:2.
26. *"rejoice and blossom."* Isaiah 35:1.

CHAPTER SEVEN

HOME WRECKER

John the Baptizer readied people for the shock of Jesus through a cleansing bath called "baptism." "Get washed up and ready for the Messiah!"[1] When you join a fraternity, they give you a pin and a secret handshake. When you join on with Jesus, you get stripped naked, thrown in the pool, washed, half drowned, and required to revert and be born again. What does that tell you? Messiah is someone so demanding, so different, that one must be detoxified from old attachments and come clean in order to receive him.

To those who took comfort in the old order, boasting of their memberships in God's chosen people saying, "My family founded this church" or, "I'm not very religious but I'm really, really spiritual," John sneered, "Don't say to yourselves 'I'm a dues-paying member! I've got Abraham and Sarah as my parents!' God can raise up a family from the stones in this river if God's people won't turn, return, be washed, and get with the revolution!"[2]

God is determined to have a family.

Look, I love my family. Why shouldn't I? They look just like me. But "family values" is not Jesus' thing. We know all about the prophet Mohammed's kin; we know next to nothing about the family of Jesus. Though Mark says that Jesus had four brothers and several sisters,[3] Jesus' family plays a remarkably negligible role in his story. Jesus' strange paternity made his birth an embarrassment for his would-be father, Joseph.[4] Though Luke says that little Jesus "grew in wisdom and in years,"[5] that does not seem to include the wisdom to cooperate with his parents. "You didn't know that I would be about my Daddy's business?" Jesus sassily asked Joseph and Mary when they reprimanded him for making them mad with worry by hanging out at the temple and arguing theology with the experts.[6] Why, Jesus? Why focus on matters about which we couldn't care less? And why assault those values—like home, parents, and family—that we consider so valuable?

When the wine gave out at a wedding party and Mary entreated her son for help, he dissed her with, "Woman, what concern is that to you and to me?"[7] Not the right tone to take with dear old Mom.

And in his ministry, Jesus thought nothing of destroying a family business with a terse, "Follow me," demanding that these fishermen abandon their aging father in the boat and join Jesus as he wandered about with his buddies.[8] Jesus' invitation to hit the road broke the hearts of many first-century parents who were counting on the kids for help in old age.

"I have come to set a man against his father, / and a daughter against her mother," he threatened.[9] "Whoever comes to me and does not hate father and mother, and wife and children, and brothers and sisters, yes, and even life itself, cannot be my disciple,"[10] a text rarely used by the church on Mother's Day.

He called people away from their livelihoods, giving no thought to their family responsibilities.[11] Although Jesus prohibited divorce,[12] suggesting a high opinion of marriage, he called some to live without marriage.[13]

To a grieving man who asked permission to give his Dad a decent burial before hitting the road as a disciple, Jesus replied, "Follow me, and let the dead bury their own dead."[14] Who would have invented such reckless comments? Surely, they came directly from Jesus.

"Your mother and your brothers and sisters are outside, asking for you," someone said. Jesus replied, "Who? Anyone who does my will is my family."[15] To be fair, Jesus seems no more antipathetic toward family than he is toward money, success, government officials, and religious authorities. In him, everything is subordinated to his mission, nothing is more important than obedience to his heavenly Father. Still, isn't it interesting that, once again, Jesus appears to devalue that which we consider so valuable?

Perhaps this nonchalance (if not downright antipathy) toward marriage and family is part of the gospel's claim about Jesus' identity—he is God sent from God, not a person produced in the tug and pull of a human family. It may also be a piece with Jesus' penchant for assaulting many of the practices that we hold dear. There was a day when Christmas greeting cards routinely displayed pictures of the baby Jesus in the manger, Joseph and Mary standing close by. Now, our Christmas cards feature our smiling families on the slopes at Vail. Forget the baby Jesus; what most interests us is us. Most of us would do anything for our families, even kill for them. No government would dare ask us to sacrifice our children to defend the bicameral legislative system. Security for and protection of our families is now the government's chief rationale for war.

Feminist critics have noted that, in our society, women were traditionally relegated to the narrow region of domesticity, left to function in the private realm of marriage and family and virtually excluded from participation in public matters. (That makes all the more notable that Jesus commended motherhood to none of his female followers.) One of the ways in which modern, democratic government has handled religion is to declare it private, a matter of the heart, a personal perference that ought not to be displayed in public. Making faith a personal opinion insures that religion will be irrelevant to anything of importance. Jesus' apparent lack of interest in marriage and family is thus an aspect of his very public, politically charged ministry, his refusal to have his mission limited to the safety of the private and the personal.

One subject that is very, very important to most of us is sexuality—a topic of endless debate at national church assemblies and the engine that seems to drive most advertizing. Curiously, we are clueless about the sexuality of Jesus. Although he seems to have relished the company of men and women, Jesus seems to have held little interest in sex. Not that Jesus was prudish (John says he intervened in the execution of a woman caught in adultery, condemning her pious accusers more severely than her). Jesus simply had little concern for the subject that seems to consume many of us. To the thoroughly liberated, sexually unconstrained modern person for whom sexual orientation is the defining mark of humanity, Jesus' nonchalance about sex may be his strangest quality. We simply cannot imagine any fully human being who is not driven by genitalia. Our preoccupation with sex is surely a testimony to the limitations of modern imagination rather than to Jesus' undeveloped libido. Presuming to stand at the summit of human development yet descending to "doing it" like dogs, rutting like rabbits (which is probably a bit unfair to dogs and rabbits), we surely would not impress Jesus. So before you dismiss Jesus for his lack of interest in the endeavor that often most energizes us, consider that Jesus was working with a very different definition of a human being than those who help to sell soap, jeans, and male-enhancement medications. Jesus appears to have held the opinion that you and I are destined for more meaningful activity than mutual orgasm.

Our economy is driven by the desire, even the right, to buy a home, settle down somewhere, make a nest, and dwell securely in a gated community with family and friends just like us. In the end, this project is futile. The family is notoriously unstable. None of our stuff, including us, lasts. Death makes all human efforts at permanence, security, and immortality silly. All that we love, including our closest friends and family, is gradually, day by day, being wrenched from our grip. The Thief gets it all.

Thus, Jesus told a wicked little story about a successful businessman who, having accumulated a barn-bursting mass of goods, said to himself, "Soul, take it easy. You have got more than enough.[16] You are secure."

That very night, said Jesus, an angel of death came, tapped the rich man on the shoulder, and addressed him, not as the successful, secure person he thought himself to be, but rather as, "You fool!" How cruel (or is it simply truthful?) for Jesus to call achievers of "the American dream," simply "fool."

Aside to Jesus: Just can't pass up an opportunity to take a swipe at us rich folks, can you?

Jesus' earliest followers, as if in imitation of him, desired "a better country,"[17] and kept their eyes fixed on a resting place beyond present arrangements. Jesus' constant movement, his relatively brief sojourn as a human being on this earth, his frequent injunctions not to put trust in things here, now, were surely meant to teach us that nothing here is eternal. All of us—whether we follow Jesus or not—are forcibly being driven toward a departure that none of us desire—death. Death finally devours what's left after fame and fortune flee. Reputation, possessions, progeny, family all crumble to dust. Jesus warned us not to trust in stuff for our security,[18] but he could have as well said not to trust family. Nothing remains—other than what God is willing to retrieve. But because of the divine determination to have a "family," a determination that is embodied to its extremity in Jesus, we have hope that the eternal God is determined to retrieve temporary us.

Why, Jesus? Why were you so cool toward family, sexuality, and romantic attachments? Perhaps because a chief focus of Jesus' mission was to reconstitute the scattered lost sheep of Israel. He left his biological family in order to form a new family based not on genetic kinship but rather upon the gracious, barrier-breaking summons of God. Is there a connection between his convening twelve disciples and there being twelve tribes in Israel? I think so. When John the Baptizer introduced Jesus, he told the smug and condescending religious leaders of Israel that, if they did not change their ways and join up with the Jesus movement, God could "from these stones . . . raise up children."[19] If those who are first called to be part of the family reject or lapse in that vocation, then God will turn to the outcasts, the lost and the marginalized. Little wonder that a persistent accusation against Jesus was, "This man welcomes sinners and eats with them."[20] He practiced a scandalously open-handed table fellowship, calling the lost and orphaned back home. Even as he was dying in agony on the cross (a gruesome form of punishment that Romans enjoyed applying to difficult-to-manage Jews), Jesus invited an outcast—a somewhat repentant thief—to join him in paradise.[21] In all these actions, and in his stories of seeking for the Lost Sheep, the Lost Coin, the Lost Boy,[22] Jesus is forming a new family composed, in great part, of those who had difficulty fitting into their human families.

Even on the cross, Jesus once again gets into it with his mother. "Woman, here is your son," he says to her.[23] Mary, look at the child you are losing, the son who you are giving over for the sins of the world. Mary was paying a high price for bearing the Son of God. It was predicted. When Jesus was born, old Simeon had foretold to Mary, "A sword will pierce your own soul too."[24] From the first, it was not easy being mother to the Son of God. And even from the cross, Jesus was busy ripping apart families and breaking the hearts of mothers. Because he was obedient to the will of God, because Jesus did not waver from his God-ordained mission, he was a great pain to his family. "Woman, behold thy son."

Then, looking at his disciple John, Jesus says, "Son, behold your mother." I expect that Jesus isn't saying, "John, do me a favor and look after Mom when I'm gone." Jesus is saying, "Mother, I'm giving you a new son. 'Son,' behold your new 'mother'." He who destroyed so many families is, on the cross, creating a new family. He who sired no children is birthing progeny that would quickly stretch the earth from end to end, encompassing all in its reach. Jesus' family is called "church."

Thus, when someone steps up and answers Jesus' call to follow him, the church washes that person in water—baptism—which says, among other things, that the person has been reborn, has started over, and has been

Aside to Jesus: You know, don't you, that today's younger generations are decidedly suspicious of institutions and organizations? They like you but don't care for your body, the church. That you became a new family, that you located among a gathering of sinners, that you made the poor, old church to be a sign of you in the world may be the most difficult thing for them to believe about you.

adopted into a new God-formed family. It is as if the person gets a new name, "Christian," that takes precedence over the person's family name. It is as if the person has already died to old attachments and former relationships and has already been raised to new life. The church is that fresh, new family that is composed of those who have heard Jesus' "follow me" and have stepped forward and said "yes." The chief act of Christian worship is not some mysterious, dark, esoteric rite. It is a family meal with everyone around the table, the Sunday dinner we call the Lord's Supper, family as God intended family to be.

What do you have to do to be credibly called a Christian, a contemporary follower of Jesus? You must be willing to be baptized, to be adopted by a new, far-flung, barrier-breaking family, the church. You must be disposed to let go of your innate American rugged individualism and be subsumed in a family bigger and more demanding than the one into which you were born. You must join us at the table, addressing some of the most sinful, often difficult-to-bear rascals as "brother" or "sister," just because Jesus loves them to death.

So you can see why, when the Jesus movement got going as the church, baptism became the radical rite of Christian initiation. Baptism not only signified everything that water means—cleansing, birth, death, refreshment, renewal, life—but baptism also meant adoption.[25] As John the Baptizer said, God is going to have a family, even if God has to raise a people out of the rocks in the river. To become a Christian, to have your life taken over by Jesus, is to be joined into a family, a people convened by "water and Spirit,"[26] a family bigger and better than your biological family, a world-wide, barrier-breaking family that goes by the name, "body of Christ."[27]

Having been deserted by most of his family, the crucified Jesus, in a last, wild act of desperate inclusion, invited a thief to join him in paradise—a stunningly defiant rebuke to the ways the world gathers people. Only a Savior like Jesus would parade into Paradise arm-in-arm with a criminal, some great trophy for his painful rescue operation for humanity. Today, every time the family of God gathers for Holy Communion, Eucharist, the Lord's Supper, a covered-dish fellowship supper, or serves soup to the homeless on the street corner, the world looks at this odd family and says, "Jesus is hanging out with the same reprobates who got him crucified."

Thank God.

YOU CAN LOOK IT UP

1. *"for the Messiah!"* Luke 3:3, paraphrased.

2. *"the revolution!"* Luke 3:8-9, paraphrased.

3. *and several sisters,* Mark 6.

4. *father, Joseph.* Matthew 1:18ff.

5. *"wisdom and in years,"* Luke 2:52.

6. *with the experts.* Luke 2:49.

7. *"you and to me?"* John 2:4.

8. *with his buddies.* Matthew 4:19.

9. *he threatened.* Matthew 10:35.

10. *"be my disciple,"* Luke 14:26.

11. *family responsibilities.* Mark 1:16-20.

12. *prohibited divorce,* 1 Corinthians 7:20; Mark 10:2-9; Luke 16:18.

13. *without marriage.* Matthew 19:11-12.

14. *"bury their own dead."* Matthew 8:22.

15. *"is my family."* Mark 3:32-35, paraphrased.

16. *more than enough.* Mark 6:43; 8:19.

17. *"a better country."* Hebrews 11:16.

18. *for our security,* Luke 10:4.

19. *"raise up children."* Luke 3:8.

20. *"eats with them."* Mark 2:16, paraphrased.

21. *in paradise.* Luke 23:43.

22. *the Lost Boy,* Luke 14.

23. *he says to her.* John 19:26.

24. *"pierce your own soul too."* Luke 2:35.

25. *meant adoption.* Galatians 4:5.

26. *"water and Spirit,"* John 3:5.

27. *"body of Christ."* 1 Corinthians 12:12.

CHAPTER EIGHT

SAVIOR

A landowner was afflicted with deadbeat tenants whose rents were ridiculously in arrears.[1] The landlord made repeated attempts to collect the rents. The wicked tenants roughed up the collection agents and sent them packing. Finally, in complete desperation but with full determination, the landlord sent his own son to collect what was his due. The renters killed the son.

Jesus' parable is a revelation of what God is up to. The Creator, having waited for us to come back home like the Prodigal Son, and having tried various devices (giving the law, sending the prophets), decided to risk all and send the Son out to the far country to rescue us from ourselves. God was determined to send us a personally addressed letter of love. And we responded, "Return to sender."

As Paul put it in a great hymn about Jesus: "Though he was in the form of God, / [he] did not regard equality with God as something to be exploited, / but emptied himself, / taking the form of a slave, / being born in human likeness."[2] God as a slave? All of this Jesus did in love for us and our salvation. Jesus saves.

At the beginning of Matthew's Gospel, an angel tells poor, befuddled, taciturn Joseph that he is to name his baby, "Jesus." Why? Because he "will save his people from their sins."[3] "To save" means, in the Greek, everything from "rescue," or "liberate," to "heal," or "comfort." God not only loves us but risks, comes to us, saves. "Salvation" is the name for what God is doing in Christ.

Old Zechariah is filled with the Holy Spirit when he sees baby John, cousin of Jesus, and sings of "a mighty savior for us" arising in Israel, a new king, "to give knowledge of salvation to his people by the forgiveness of their sins," through the tender mercy of our God, when the day shall dawn upon us from on high.[4] Jesus saves.

John said that if he had put everything Jesus said and did into his Gospel, all the books in the world couldn't contain it.[5] While this has to be an exaggeration, the gospels are amazingly concise and crisp. Only what is important has been said. You could get everything they say about Jesus into a copy of *USA Today* with plenty of space to spare. John says that he has told us just enough for us to believe that Jesus is Savior, the complete answer to what's wrong with us and the world. It's as if the gospels are saying that all you really need to know about Jesus is the bare essentials—Jesus saves.

Why, Jesus? Why did your ministry end in a cross rather than a crown? Jesus got into all manner of trouble because of whom he saved. Jesus saved people who nobody thought could be saved or even wanted saved. "This man welcomes sinners and eats with them!" we repeatedly have heard his critics whine.[6] Because he not only welcomed sinners to his table (which would have been controversial enough) but also actively sought them, Jesus was crucified. To outcasts who thought that God had said no to them, Jesus was God's great yes.[7] He constantly dined with his most severe critics. He partied with people nobody would have wanted to spend a Saturday night with. At the end, with whom did he share his Last Supper? Sinners who just happened to be his closest friends. And in his resurrection, with whom did he dine at his post-Easter meals? Sinners.[8] His door was too wide to suit many of the faithful.

Once upon a time, a farmer went forth to sow and did what: carefully, meticulously prepared the ground, removed all the rocks and weeds, and sowed one seed six inches from another? No. The farmer, without preparation, just went out and began to sling the seed.[9] This is farming Jesus-style. A dragnet full of creatures "both good and bad" is hauled into the boat. Should the catch be sorted, separating the valuable from the worthless? No.[10] The Master is more impressed with the size of the haul than with the quality of the harvest. One day, not today, it will all be sorted. A field is planted with good seed. But a perverse enemy sows weeds in the field. Cull the wheat from the weeds? No. Someday he will judge good from bad, but we are not to bother ourselves with such sorting. The Master seems to find more joy in careless sowing, miraculous growing, and reckless harvesting than in taxonomy of the good from the bad, the worthwhile from the worthless, the saved from the damned.

"Which one of you?" Jesus asks,[11] "having lost a sheep will you not leave the 99 sheep to fend for themselves in the wilderness and beat the bushes until you find the one lost sheep? Which one of you will not put that sheep on your shoulders like a recovered lost child and say to your friends, 'Come party with me'? Which one of you would not do that?"

"Which of you women," Jesus continues, "if you lose a quarter would not rip up the carpet and strip the house bare and when you have found your lost coin run into the street and call to your neighbors, 'Come party with me, I found my quarter!' Which one of you would not do that?"

And which of you fathers, having two sons, the younger of whom leaves home, blows all your money, and then comes dragging back in rags, would not throw the biggest bash this town has ever seen, singing, "This son of mine was dead but is now alive!" Which one of you would not do that?

And which of you, journeying down the Jericho Road, upon seeing a complete stranger lying in the ditch half dead, bleeding, would not risk your life, put the injured man in the backseat of your Jaguar, take him to the hospital, spend every dime you have and more on his recovery?. Which one of you would not do that?

The answer is that *none of us* would behave in this unseemly, reckless, extravagant way. But these are not stories about us. These are God's stories: God the searching shepherd, the careless farmer, the undiscerning fisherman, the reckless woman, the extravagant father, the prodigal Samaritan. Jesus reveals a God who is no reticent, reclusive deity. This God comes out to seek and to save the lost.

In the parable of the Lost Boy,[12] when the boy was "yet far off" the father ran to welcome his Prodigal Son. The son, perhaps hoping to ameliorate some of his father's just wrath, had a penitent speech prepared for his homecoming,. The father disallowed the son even to speak. Holding nothing back, running to the son, the father embraced him, welcomed him not simply back home but to an extravagant party, treating him not as the wayward son he was, but with royal gifts of ring, shoes, and robe, treating him as the prince the father intended him to be.

Who is God? Jesus says: God is the Father who ran to embrace his once lost son and invite him to a party.

Jesus begins his famous sermon with, "Blessed are you who are poor, for yours is the kingdom of God."[13] To those who can't buy the kingdom, he gives it for nothing. Matthew is not spiritualizing the Beatitudes when he adds to poor the words "in spirit."[14] Poor is poor. To those who haven't got much spirit, to those who are inept in spiritual matters, to those whose eyes glaze over when reading a book about Jesus, to those who can do little to

> Aside to Jesus: I'm not all that surprised that you would love me and my friends, and even dare to die for us. What surprises me is that you love my neighbor—yes, the one who plays rap music, keeps a pit bull, and possesses Neanderthal political opinions, that one!—as much as you love and save me.

further their case before God, who, by their poverty, have no control over their future, Jesus promises everything, his whole glorious kingdom.[15]

Remember that another of the names given to Jesus at his birth was "Immanuel," that is, "God with us." With all our limitations and false motives, we can't come to God. We don't have to. In Jesus the Christ, God comes to us. And Paul says that if you look at this crucified one and exclaim, "Hey, that's God with us!" it's because God has given you the gift of faith, the grace of belief.[16] Even your faith in Jesus is a result of the saving work of Jesus.

Luke tells this one: Jesus parades through Jericho with his disciples one day, on his way to Jerusalem.[17] Among the curious crowd, Jesus spots Zacchaeus, a sleazy, short chief tax collector. Jesus, never one to pass up an opportunity for a free meal at the wrong place, promptly invites himself to dinner at the old reprobate's house, once again intruding, pushing in where he is not wanted. (Luke is generally rough on the rich, so it's odd to have his as the sole report that when Jesus went to Jericho, he went to no house except that of a rich man.)

Zacchaeus wasn't just a "tax collector," that is, a lackey for the oppressive Romans, financier of state-sponsored terrorism against his fellow Jews; he was the chief tax collector. He was not only a robber; he was rich. And he was the only person with whom Jesus feasted when Jesus came to Jericho.

So just in case you didn't get the joke back in Luke 15 after parties were thrown for the salvation of the stupid lost sheep, the worthless lost dime, and the profligate lost boy, Luke rubs our collective nose in it one more time: a dinner party with Hitler's henchman in Jericho. When we (again) grumbled, "He's gone to be the guest of a man who is a sinner!" Jesus responded (again), "Like I told you in Luke 15, the Son of Man came to seek and to save the lost. When are you pious people going to get it through your thick heads that I came to seek and to save the lost?"

Back in Luke 15, the problem was "this fellow welcomes sinners and eats with them."[18] Here, it's, "He has gone to be the guest of one who is a sinner."[19] And Jesus said to us grumblers (once again, it wasn't the "sinners" like Zacchaeus but the "righteous" like me who murmured against Jesus' chosen companions), "Today salvation has come to this house."[20]

Why Jesus? Because Jesus saves. So here's a definition of "salvation" as Christians define the word: salvation is whenever Jesus intrudes into your space, whenever Jesus makes your sinful table the site of his salvation feast. Salvation is what Jesus did for Zacchaeus. Zacchaeus didn't invite Jesus to dinner. Jesus invited himself. Hardly anyone in Scripture chooses Jesus or decides to be saved by him. As we have noted, the gospel is a story about Jesus' choices and decisions for the lost, not our choices and decisions for Jesus. That's why we grumbled, still do. "He has gone in to be the guest of a sinner!" when we ought to be exclaiming, "I can't believe that you have come to the house of a sinner like me!"

For all I know, Zacchaeus may have grumbled about this wandering, uninvited dinner guest who took over the party. Yet Zacchaeus eventually gets so carried away because Jesus has invited himself to Zacchaeus' home that, when the glasses of Mogen David are raised, Zacchaeus toasts his rabbinical guest with, "And just to show you how great it is for me to have a smart rabbi like you in our home, I'm going to give half of all I've got to the poor, and if it can be shown that I have defrauded anyone of anything, I'll restore it, I'll . . ."

Jesus laughs, "*If* it can be shown that you have defrauded anybody? Get real, Zach! All Jericho knows that you've stolen from *everybody*. You're a tax collector, for God's sake, *chief* tax collector, the god-father of all the defrauders of everybody!"

Then Jesus, having taken some of the wind out of Zacchaeus, saids, "Today salvation has come to this house, . . . for the Son of man came to seek and to save the lost."

"Did you say 'lost'?" asks Zacchaeus. "I'll admit that I've made a few financial mistakes, and sometimes I got a bit carried away in the performance of my governmental duties, but 'lost'? Don't you think that's overstating things? Look at this crystal, these drapes. Check out my tax return from last year, and see if that looks 'lost' to you."

Once again, if Jesus had some odd notions of "salvation," he had odder ideas of who is "lost" and who should be found. Salvation is not something that we do; it is what Jesus does. In salvation, the one who says, "I, I, I," learns to exclaim to Jesus, "You, you, you." What a kingdom where the main requirement for membership is to be honest-to-God lost, and the main claim of citizenship is not to have discovered but to have been found!

And we, the righteous, the insiders, those well-schooled in the faith, those of us in the theological know, hated him for it. After this little episode at the Zacchaeus mansion, we righteous grumblers got organized. The next chapter of Luke finds Jesus up the road in Jerusalem, on his way to a cross, where he would be nailed there by the lost, dying only *for* the lost.

There is, thus, in Jesus a kind of relentless divine reach. I guess that's why the church, which believes that Jesus saves, has been reluctant to say for sure whether or not Jesus saves people who are not in the church. The church's reluctance about this matter is not due to the church's mushy inclusiveness but rather to the church's disinclination to set limits on just what the love of Jesus can and can't do. Just when

> Aside to Jesus: Among the many offensive, inappropriate, abrasive comments you made, surely this quip about whores is the most distasteful of all—to us good church folks.

I settle in and try to reduce Jesus' love to me and my friends huddled in church, I hear him say to (us) the faithful, "The tax-collectors and the prostitutes are going into the kingdom of God ahead of you!"[21]

Paul preaches that, in Christ, God wants something even more sweeping than the rescue of a few sinners. Writing some years before the earliest of the gospels, Paul says that God's ultimate desire is restoration of all things in Christ, things above and below, near and far, a whole new world: in him, we have redemption through his blood, the forgiveness of our trespasses, according to the riches of his grace that he lavished upon us. . . . He has been made known to us to unite all things in him, "things in heaven and things on earth."[22]

All things. Picture Paul preaching this bodacious, universal claim to a cluster of Christians huddled together at their church in Colossae: he is the image of the invisible God, the firstborn of all creation. In him, all things were created, in heaven and on earth, visible and invisible, whether thrones or dominions or principalities or authorities—all things were created through him and for him. In him, all things hold together. "For in him all the fullness of God was pleased to dwell, and through him God was pleased to reconcile to himself all things, whether on earth or in heaven, by making peace by the blood of his cross."[23]

There is a universality in Jesus as he spoke of God's rain falling upon the heads of the just and unjust, God's sun shining warmly upon the good and the bad, blurring all our neat distinctions between who is in and who is out. All. While his expectations for his first disciples were demanding and exacting, Jesus' criteria for selection of his disciples were notoriously expansive and lax. He invited all. This thing with Jesus is more than personal, individual, or private. It's cosmic, sweeping, and universal. "All things."

In John's Gospel, Jesus said, "I, when I am lifted up from the earth, will draw all people to myself."[24] Like a great magnet that indiscriminately picks up all kinds of metallic trash, Jesus says that when he is lifted up (and how he was lifted up!) he will extravagantly draw all to himself. All. Stand at the foot of the cross, and you will see Jesus' magnetic pull of all unto himself. As a pastor, I've seen people slip through the cracks, ripped violently through the eye of the needle, caught in the great dragnet, cut down and gathered for the harvest, pursued all the way into the wilderness, drawn unto him, invited. It is, for me, living proof that God was in Christ and reconciling the whole wide world. All.

One day, Jesus' disciples complained, "We saw an uncredentialed exorcist who, though he did some good, was not one of us."

Jesus casually replied, "Don't stop him. If he's not against us, he's for us."[25] Elsewhere, just after Jesus told his disciples that he had personally selected them for his flock, he said, "I have sheep that do not belong to this fold. I must bring them in also."[26] What did he mean by that? Could there be others who—even though they are not yet in the church, even though they have not yet heard the gospel, and not yet said yes to Jesus—are still beloved, though incognito, making them incipient sheep of his fold? Knowing something of the expansiveness and reach of Jesus' love, I think it's likely.

Sometimes people ask questions like, "Is it possible that even Hindus will be saved?" Note first that this is a question of no interest in the New Testament. The stunning thing to Paul is not how few will eventually be caught in the great dragnet of divine grace but how many. All. Early

Christian writers seemed to have little interest in limiting the scope of God's gracious reach. Can it be that "lost" simply means that, up to now, you haven't yet been found, but one day you probably will be? Note also that salvation is what God does and, as we have seen in Jesus, God saves. Finally, note that salvation is God's business, not ours. Most Christians feel that if God could find a way to get to them, to bring them home, to make them whole, to turn them around, well, God can save just about anybody.

Paul says that what happened to Jesus on Easter continues as believers are "made alive" in Christ:

> who is rich in mercy, out of the great love with which he loved us even when we were dead through our trespasses, made us alive together with Christ—by grace you have been saved—and raised us up with him and seated us with him in the heavenly places in Christ Jesus, so that in the ages to come he might show the immeasurable riches of his grace in kindness toward us in Christ Jesus. For by grace you have been saved through faith, and this is not your own doing; it is the gift of God.[27]

The church is called by Paul the "first fruits"[28] of the great worldwide harvest, the vanguard, the initial results of the dragnet of salvation, a clue to what God shall one day, somehow, do for all of creation. When Christians gather to worship on Sunday, assembled on the basis of nothing more than the embrace of God, we say and sing, "This is the world's ultimate destiny, this is how it will all look once God is all in all and the kingdom comes."

YOU CAN LOOK IT UP

1. *in arrears.* Matthew 21:34 ff.
2. *"in human likeness."* Philippians 2:6-7.
3. *"from their sins."* Matthew 1:21.
4. *"from on high."* Luke 1:69, 77.
5. *contain it.* John 21:5.
6. *his critics whine.* Luke 15:2.
7. *God's great yes.* 2 Corinthians 1:20.
8. *meals? Sinners.* Luke 24:13-35.
9. *sling the seed.* Matthew 13:18.
10. *worthless? No.* Matthew 13:47.
11. *"you?" Jesus asks,* Luke 15 ff.
12. *the Lost Boy,* Luke 15.
13. *"kingdom of God."* Luke 6:20.
14. *the words "in spirit."* Matthew 5:3.
15. *whole glorious kingdom.* Matthew 5:3.
16. *grace of belief.* Ephesians 2:8.
17. *way to Jerusalem.* Luke 19:1-10.
18. *"eats with them."* Luke 15:2.
19. *"guest of one who is a sinner."* Luke. 19:7.
20. *"to this house."* Luke 19:9.
21. *"ahead of you!"* Matthew 21:31.
22. *things on earth.* Ephesians 1:7-10.
23. *of his cross.* Colossians 1:19-20.
24. *"all people to myself."* John 12:32.
25. *"he's for us."* Mark 9:38-41.
26. *"them in also."* John 10:16.
27. *gift of God.* Ephesians 2:4-9.
28. *the "first fruits,"* 1 Corinthians 15:20.

CHAPTER NINE

SOVEREIGN

When the angel Gabriel told Mary that she was to have a baby, Gabriel promised that her baby would grow up royal: "The Lord God will give him the throne of his ancestor David. He will reign over the house of Jacob forever, and of his kingdom there will be no end."[1] Israel had not had much of a king since Solomon, son of David. At last, a real king for the house of David. Israel would be back on top.

Surprisingly, when Jesus began his work, he prepared not in an exclusive prep school for royals but by being cast into the wilderness.[2] Alone in a trackless, wild place, hungry after a forty-day fast, Jesus faced off with the Tempter. (In my experience, most significant temptation occurs early in a person's career.) Satan's challenges were of a particular kind, considerably more alluring than a bottle of booze or a night on the town: "If you are really the Son of God, then act as God is supposed to act: (1) feed the hungry by miraculously turning stones into bread, (2) throw yourself down from the temple tower and walk away unhurt in a spectacular feat of supernatural power, or (3) take charge of all the kingdoms of the world."

Even though Satan backed up his offers with Scripture (didn't God provide miraculous bread for Israel wandering in the wilderness?),[3] Jesus refused. Unlike the primal parents, Adam and Eve, who were tempted by food (eating the fruit of the forbidden tree), hungry Jesus said, "No!" He resisted the temptation to be other than who he was called to be. The temptations are not just any old allurement. The temptations were all related to Jesus' identity as Messiah ("If you are . . ."). Jesus is first known not in what he affirms but by what he rejects, not by the good he does but in the otherwise good he refuses. He will not fulfill the world's expectations for God. Repudiating miraculous displays of power, glory, and supernatural proficiency, Jesus said, "No."

We, who are so enamored of politicians and their potency, marvel that Jesus rebuffed Satan's offer of a political career. Taking Jesus up to a high summit, Satan said, "Here are all the kingdoms of the world in their glory. I can give them to whomever I want, for they have been given to me. If you are the long-awaited Messiah, act like it. All you must do is to worship me."

Jesus said, "No." Satan slinked away until "a more opportune time."

Who gave the world's kingdoms to Satan? Did, at some point, God say, "Politics? Not interested. Satan, here are the kingdoms of the world. Have fun with all your bigwig political cronies"? Is a link being forged here between politics and worship of Satan?

Since nobody was there in the wilderness but Satan and Jesus, I assume Jesus must have reported all this to his followers himself, perhaps so that they might steel themselves against the lures of Satan. To tell the truth, many of Jesus' later followers yielded to the temptations which he resisted. How could we claim to be speaking in the name of the one who resisted the temptation to coerce, bedazzle, and overwhelm the world yet launch "crusades" to "win souls," as we swagger about in his name? Sometimes church folks are guilty of a "savior complex," as if it were up to us and our extraordinary efforts to save the world and make everyone else do right. Odd to find so little of the egotistical "savior complex" in Jesus!

I admit that Jesus rejected everything for which I would give my right arm. At times, when I get aggravated at the slow, virtually imperceptible, growth of the kingdom or God's apparent tardiness to rush to deliver me from whatever it is I demand to be rescued from in order to make it through the night, I hear Satan's very words of temptation to Jesus emanating from my own lips. "If you are truly the Son of God, give me what I want, now!"

Mark tells a different story of Jesus' temptation in the wilderness. Mark says cryptically that Jesus was in the wilderness alone with "wild beasts."[4] What is that supposed to mean?

Perhaps Mark is thinking about the promise of the poetic prophet Isaiah: a king will come who will be a servant (not the way we normally think of kings.) In that day, a new administration of the Servant will rule the whole wide world. The nations, the sources of so much violence, will at last be at peace. The earth will be transformed in God's great ecological restoration. The wild, desiccated desert shall blossom. Wolves will lie peacefully with lambs, wild leopards will cavort with young goats, and "a little child will lead them." The earth will be full of the true knowledge of God, like the waters of the sea.[5] And a little child will be in charge. After people got to know Jesus, they recalled this text, linking it to his curious sovereignty.

Those "wild beasts" with Jesus out in the wilderness may be Mark's way of saying that we are on the verge of the promised day, when the wolf will lie with the lamb and a "little child" will lead. The whole world will be put right, and nature, instead of being the home of tooth, claw, and nail cruelty, will become a place of harmony.

Why Jesus? Because many people—especially the poor, hungry, sick, imprisoned, or rejected—yearn for a different, better world. People on the bottom are usually the first to know that, despite the administration's cheerful press releases, something is wrong. In his parables of the kingdom, Jesus promises that hoped-for transformation. He names it "the kingdom of God" (in Matthew, "the kingdom of heaven"). Many in Israel longed for this world to look more explicitly like God's world. Though God created the world and called it "good,"[6] a good world is not what God got. Injustice, cruelty, sickness, and death abound. I hope that you may be blessed with the good sense to feel, however inchoately, that this world, as it is, is not as good as it gets.

God's great rescue operation for a fallen world is Jesus Christ. The great end of that venture is the kingdom of God, that time and place when God, at last, gets what God wants. Many want a better world, a closer, more heightened sense of God's nearness and God's rule, but it is one thing to anticipate such a time and place; it is quite another actually to look at this lowly Jew from Nazareth, the Servant, and believe that, in him, the kingdom has come here, now.

Jesus burst upon the scene preaching the kingdom's arrival: now is the hour of salvation![7] Let go of everything and get on board God's reign, now, here![8] Wake up![9] "Be dressed for action and have your lamps lit," Jesus warned.[10] Turn around ("repent"), change your ways, or else appear stupidly out of step with reality now that the King is here and the kingdom is now.[11]

The Romans tended to be tolerant pluralists, in their own way, allowing and even encouraging their subjects to worship as many gods as they pleased. Jews like Jesus proved to be particularly exasperating with their dogged, exclusivistic determination that there is one God, and God is the one and only deity who is jealous of all rivals. During Jesus' childhood, a revolutionary named Judas the Galilean launched a revolt in Judea under the slogan, "no master but God." That's the kingdom of God in a nutshell—we serve nobody but God. You can certainly see why Jesus attracted the attention of the authorities and why they eventually attempted to shut him up.

Luke says that, when Jesus was born, the first to get the news were poor shepherds working the night shift.[12] Matthew remembers strange Gentile magi from the East offering rich treasures to the new "king."[13] Their accounts, taken together, are a politically charged announcement of an all-embracing kingdom that breaks down the power structures upon which all worldly kingdoms are built: the rich ruling over the poor, the homefolks protected from foreigners, Caesar swaggering like a god, and the military serving as the sole means of national security.

A major cause of friction between Jesus and the religious establishment was not that he preached the kingdom of heaven (many in Israel hoped for as much) but rather that he proclaimed that kingdom here and now. In Jesus, anticipation and expectation are announced as reality, as a demand to join in and join up. A major way of getting rid of Jesus is to keep Jesus vague, a sort of spiritual possibility. When the Jesus who once was relegated to the realm of an historical figure or a fuzzy spiritual feeling takes up room, stakes a claim, and becomes the demanding one standing beside you, commanding you, here and now—well . . .

"What is the kingdom of God like?" Jesus asked as lead-in to many parables. "It is like a mustard seed that someone took and sowed in a garden; it grew and became a tree, and the birds of the air made nests in its branches."[14] The kingdom of God is not the result of earnest human effort; it is what God does. God's triumph comes as surely as harvest follows seedtime. Yet the kingdom comes surprisingly, starting out ridiculously small.

The kingdom of God not only means power, God's power active on earth, but also God's empowerment of ordinary women and men to be agents of God's sovereignty. Though Jesus' talk of taking over the world by employment of a trifling gaggle of disciples or through the sweet old folks who gather in his name at St. John's on the Expressway may seem ridiculous (as silly as a tree from a mustard seed), it is through such preposterously small measures that God miraculously grows a cosmic kingdom.

"Blessed are the eyes that see what you see! For I tell you that many prophets and kings desired to see what you see, but did not see it, and to hear what you hear, but did not hear it,"[15] Jesus told his followers, vanguard of the kingdom. Despite Jesus' enthusiasm for the outbreak of God's reign, many looked at the results of his ministry and found them too meager to deserve the designation "messianic." "The kingdom of God is not coming with things that can be observed; nor will they say, 'Look, here it is!' or 'There it is!' . . . The kingdom of God is among you,"[16] warned Jesus, with a touch of defensiveness in his voice. Jesus' identity, Jesus' reign as victor is not self-evident. His victory, here, now, is open to a number of interpretations.

It's a wonder that anybody looked at Jesus and the rather measly results of his ministry and exclaimed, "He's a king!" Yet some did—a few women, ex-tax collectors, and former fisherfolk, the very young and the very old, along with many untouchables and undesirables. Their comprehension of his reign was so against the way we think about things that their acclamation of Jesus was itself a wonder. Thus, the church has always regarded faith in Jesus, that is, trust that he is who he says he is, as a gift of God. On one occasion, Jesus even thanked his heavenly Father that he had hidden

> Aside to Jesus: Assuming that some of the young and the foolish have gotten this far in this book, I sure hope that you are giving them the faith to believe that what I'm saying about you, despite my limitations in saying it, just may be the truth about you. I can't write this book by myself.

his true royal identity from the wise and the discerning and had given it only to the young and the foolish.[17]

"The kingdom of God is like . . ." begins many a Jesus story. It is as if, in these stories, Jesus gropes for a proper analogy from everyday human life to describe something strange and against our presuppositions. "The kingdom of God is as if someone would scatter seed on the ground, and would sleep and rise night and day, and the seed would sprout and grow, he does not know how."[18] God's triumph comes, but not through our earnest efforts. The reign of God is a miraculous gift of God. Here. Now.

Jesus encouraged no hope for a national messiah to arise from the family of David to assume worldly political power, nor did he proclaim himself as such. He criticized efforts by some (the Pharisees) to turn the kingdom into the preserve of pious adherents to the Law.[19] Membership in the kingdom is not limited to those with enough leisure and resources to sit around thinking spiritual thoughts; it's accessible for all, particularly those whom many of the presumed righteous exclude by their rules and rituals. Jesus simply announced that God is present, that God is already establishing God's rule. God is no longer trapped in God's own glory; God is sovereign, home wrecker, and Savior here, now.

Paul says that in being "raised from the dead," Jesus "disarmed the rulers and authorities and made a public example of them, triumphing over them."[20] In defeating death, Jesus now rules: "God put this power to work in Christ when he raised him from the dead and seated him at his right hand in the heavenly places, far above all rule and authority and power and dominion, and above every name that is named, not only in this age but also in the age to come."[21]

When will God's glorious rescue operation and reign be fully accomplished? Matthew, Mark, and Luke all record Jesus saying, "there are some standing here who will not taste death until they see that the kingdom of God has come with power."[22] If Jesus meant that the promised transformation of the world would take place right away, it didn't happen. This apparent delay of the end and the concomitant return of Christ in glory concerned many. Second Peter urges his fellow early Christians to hang on. With God, a thousand years are like one of our days; Jesus will come back soon.[23]

The continued sorry state of the world, Caesar's prolonged, bullying swagger about the earth, the surfeit of suffering and misery don't look much like the "kingdom of heaven." Many continue to respond to the claim, "Jesus Christ is Lord!" with, "But with all the suffering and heartache in the world, how can you say . . . ?" They have their point. The incompletion of the kingdom, or its slow, often imperceptible, advent among us is still a major impediment to faith in Jesus. Nietzsche scoffed at Christians of his day, saying, "You'll have to look a great deal more redeemed if I am to believe in your Redeemer."

What most of the church decided about the timing of the kingdom's coming was that Jesus' words and deeds, as responded to in the church, were visible proof that a once accustomed, secure world had ended and the promised transformation of the world had already begun. An old world was losing its grip; a new world is being born. Though the kingdom is not fully, completely come, there's enough of the kingdom to live with joy and transformed lives right now. Yet the fullness of the reign is still to come, so Christians live with the eager expectation that there is more.

Few Christians worry much about the precise date for that complete transformation. Jesus squelched such speculation, saying, "About that day or hour no one knows, neither the angels in heaven, nor the Son, but only the Father."[24] Most Christians believe that they have had glimpses of the outbreak of the kingdom on many Sundays in the gathering of the church around God's table, or in works of love and mercy in the world. Any time that God's will is done on earth, it's as if we're seeing visible confirmation of our prayer, "thy kingdom come, thy will be done on earth as it is in heaven."

Most great, world-changing revolutionaries talk about the end of the world. Jesus was no exception, though his talk of the world's end had his own twist. In Jesus' talk of a final cataclysm, Jesus wasn't exactly saying that the world was coming to an end. Rather, he was claiming, with vivid speech and bold assertion, that Rome's rule over the world was coming to an end (which would have no doubt seemed like the end of the world for many people who thought too highly of the empire). "Give up your agenda and take up mine" was his kingdom message. Or, as he put it, "repent and believe the good news." It wasn't escapist; it was revolutionary. "Repent" thus means to abandon your own allegiances and join up with us. Be more revolutionary, even than your hoped-for revolutions.

Jesus didn't simply talk about the kingdom; he got it rolling. He was little David facing down Goliath with the only weapons God gave—sacrificial, suffering love. Jesus never discounts the pain produced by the evils around him and nowhere attempts to explain or rationalize evil. Tragedy happens; misfortune blows where it will.

With Jesus' welcome to the kingdom also came a warning: people must "repent," that is, exchange their agendas for God's. They must change their ways and sign on for the new kingdom or else. You knew you were part of the kingdom not because you felt differently in your heart but rather because you lived differently. People could see that the kingdom of God was not just "in you," as a subjective attitude, but rather "among you," as a recognizably changed allegiance. Sign up, sell off, and join Jesus on the road.

If they didn't, Jesus the prophet warned, like Israel's great prophets, there would be hell to pay. There are always consequences for refusing to go with God, refusing to get on board with God's plans for the rescue of the world.[25] For one thing, the Romans were not going to put up for one minute with a violent Jewish revolt that attempted to get a new world through the world's violent means. Rome would utterly crush Israel (which was just what happened not too long after Jesus' crucifixion). For another thing, your life and your world will continue to be sadly out of sync as you continue to dance to the music of fake gods and follow false saviors.

Not a new religion, a different moral code, some fuzzy spiritual experience, a set of new doctrines, or a plan for individual salvation, kingdom talk was about Israel at last coming to fruition, Israel at last becoming what God had always intended—the kingdom of God, though not in a way that most people expected. A whole new world. That's why Jesus spoke so often in the future tense: mourners *will be* comforted; the hungry *will be* filled. He spoke of a grand reality that was not yet fully present, not yet completely evident. Thus, he put us in the vulnerable position of having to follow him on the basis of promises, in the future tense rather than on the basis of hard and fast evidence. We have therefore got to be able to look for that which is not fully seen, to hope for that which is not fully present, if we are going to walk with him.

I know a woman who somehow summoned the courage to forgive the person at whose hands she had suffered a terrible wrong. When I asked how on earth she overcame her anger, her understandable desire for revenge, her just craving to hurt the one who had so hurt her, she said simply, "Jesus enabled me to forgive."

How on earth? She was, for me, visible evidence that the kingdom of heaven has indeed taken up residence on the earth—not yet fully, still incompletely—but enough for me to know when I saw it face-to-face. She must be a citizen of elsewhere.

Jesus opens his most famous sermon by announcing a topsy-turvy world:

> Blessed are you who are poor, for yours is the kingdom of God.
> Blessed are you who are hungry now, for you will be filled.
> Blessed are you who weep now, for you will laugh.[26]

"Your kingdom come!"[27] Jesus taught his disciples always to pray. Jesus' challenge was not, "How can I have a more purposeful life?" but rather, "How can I get my life aligned with God's purposes for creation?" Jesus' ethics, his way in the world, was not a means of getting into the kingdom—behave in this way and, if you perform all this well, some day you will be worthy to enter the kingdom. Rather, the basis of his moral teaching is, "This is reality now that God's kingdom has come and is coming among you, here and now. Wake up, live in the light of the facts of life."

The good news is that we don't have to wait until his reign is obvious to enjoy the revolution. In forgiving enemies, blessing those who persecute us, and in taking up the cross daily, we are not called by Jesus to be pious doormats for the world. Rather, we are taking charge in Jesus' name, joining the revolution, beginning the great turnaround toward reality that shall one day be hailed as, "the kingdom of the world has become the kingdom of our Lord" in which "he shall reign for ever and ever!"[28]

In Luke, Jesus' last words from the cross are, "Father, into your hands I commend my spirit."[29] Jesus is commending all that he did and all that he said into the hands of God. God's kingdom comes, as Jesus taught, by the action of God. It appears to be the nature of God's kingdom to win victory through suffering, sacrificial love, God weaving into God's purposes, even the worst of human sin, even the sin of crucifying God's own Son. We're not far from the kingdom whenever we commend our lives and our deeds to God.

In John's Gospel, Jesus' last words in agony on the cross are, "It is finished."[30] Christians believe that he meant not only it's over, his life was finished, but also his work was fully accomplished. Jesus' death became the great, final act of reconciliation of humanity to God, the inauguration of the kingdom. At the Last Supper, in the upper room, as Jesus shared the loaf and the cup with his disciples, he said that he would not eat and drink with them again until they ate and drank in the kingdom of God.[31] Then, on the evening of his resurrection, as Jesus took, blessed, and broke the bread at the inn at Emmaus, their eyes were opened, and they saw the risen Christ with them.[32] The kingdom toward which Jesus pointed in his parables was now an undeniable reality around the table. The mournful Last Supper had been transformed, by the risen Christ, into a great victory banquet.

The ability to see the kingdom coming reminds me of the time Jesus healed a blind man.[33] No sooner had the man received sight than a heated theological debate ensued among the crowd. Does this wonder mean that Jesus is a prophet? Is Jesus somebody better than a prophet? Can he be the Messiah?

The bedraggled blind man (if you think everybody is thrilled that a blind man can now see, you don't know much about theologians) said quietly, "Look, I don't know much about theology, but one thing I know; I once was blind, but now I see."

To this day, billions believe that Jesus is the Messiah, the Christ, the Son of God, the king of the world, despite any evidence to the contrary, not on the basis of some knock-down argument, but simply, "One thing I know is that, though I was blind, now I see."

Christians sometimes hear, "Forgiveness is noble, up to a point, as long as one remains realistic about its limits." Or, "Prayer can be powerful, even useful, but sometimes you have got to face facts and . . ." For those who have been given eyes to see the coming of the kingdom, God's promised victory, the kingdom of God is a name for an accomplished "fact," the true "reality." This is the open secret we wouldn't have known about the world without the teaching of Jesus, the world we wouldn't have been able to see without Jesus. Jesus is more than personal and private. As one early preacher put it, these things didn't happen "in a corner,"[34] This Jesus thing is cosmic. Surprise! The kingdom of God is the truth about the world all the way down.

Thus, Jesus could say, "You have heard that it was said . . . but I say to you."[35] Once adultery was defined as having sex with someone to whom you weren't married. Now, it's a matter of looking at someone lustfully.[36] (And who isn't guilty of that?) Once, a man could send his wife away just by writing a note of dismissal (a practice decidedly advantageous to lousy husbands), but this is not how God intends women and men to relate. Now that the kingdom of God is here, people must keep their promises for better or worse.[37] A better righteousness[38] is required, a righteousness that is not only based upon the commands of Jesus but also (thank God for all of us lustful lookers) the constant forgiveness of Jesus. There was a time when certain sorts of behavior made sense in the old world, but now, in the new world, with the outbreak of the kingdom of God, the proximity of God's kingdom requires a rethinking of everything. Thus, to look at Jesus and say "I believe" is to believe that this victory is true and real and to live in the light of that fact, to acquire a new passport signifying a new citizenship.

Paul called Jesus "Lord," saying, "Jesus Christ is Lord!"[39] *Lord* can mean simply "sir," though it can also mean "master," the person in charge of the servants. *Lord* can mean "ruler," as in "Jesus is the true ruler, and Caesar isn't." *Lord* was even a frequent designation for God in the Old Testament. Paul applies "Lord," in all these meanings, to Jesus. Jesus is not only a person, a man. Jesus is also God, and this one who was fully God and fully human rules. To say, "I believe that Jesus is Lord" means "I believe Jesus is in charge." Jesus rules. Even more, for the way you live your life, it means, "I believe that Jesus is Lord, therefore, Jesus is to be obeyed."

Thus, when his disciples asked, "Teach us to pray, like John the Baptist taught his disciples,"[40] Jesus responded, "When you pray, say: "Our Father in heaven, holy be your name, your will be done, your kingdom come on earth as in heaven. . . . Forgive our debts to you." And how is this prayer answered? "As we also forgive our debtors."[41]

Jesus' distinctive designation for God was not "King" or "Sovereign" but "Father." One would have thought, considering the tradition of Israel, that it would have been otherwise, because the royal image occurs so frequently in Hebrew Scripture. God, as Jesus speaks of God, does not tyrannize humanity but rather relates to it, the way a loving parent bonds with a child. God redefines our notions of divine sovereignty by being kind and merciful rather than powerful and controlling. God is "a father who has compassion for his children."[42] In Jesus, the sovereignty of God is being dramatically redefined by love.

Around 110 C.E., Pliny, Rome's man in charge of Bithinia on the Black Sea (Northern Turkey), wrote to the head office asking what to do about a little group of religious fanatics who "sing a hymn on the first day of the week to Christ as to a god." The emperor replied that, if these Christians leave it at that, what's the harm? As long as they don't cause a commotion, don't trouble yourself; they are no threat to the empire.

That was a colossal error in judgment by the emperor. In just a couple of centuries, that little band of Christians deposed the emperor and took over the empire without raising an army or firing a shot.

Oh, what a jumble of a kingdom! An upstanding member of the religious community, noted for his generous giving to charity, offered a prayer of gratitude at the temple, thanking God for rescuing him from the ranks of "thieves, rogues, [and] adulterers."[43] A long way off from the altar (a man like him can't get too close to God), a despised tax collector could only blurt out a penitent confession—it would take too long to enumerate all of his sins. "God have mercy on me, a sinner!" Then Jesus dropped the bomb: the lousy tax collector went home made "righteous," not the nice Pharisee.

A notorious woman slipped past the bouncer and crashed a party to which Jesus had been invited, and she began to make an outrageous fuss over Jesus, letting down her hair, caressing his feet, and bathing him with her tears.[44] The pious folks at the table, seeing this shamefully sensuous display, began to grumble that, if this Jesus were a real prophet he would be able to see what sort of disreputable person this woman is and give her the boot. Jesus praised the woman and bid her go on her way, her sins forgiven.

The charge that Jesus—prophet, religious teacher, biblical interpreter— was "a glutton and a drunkard, a friend of tax collectors and sinners"[45] is well documented. It was one thing to proclaim God's kingdom as coming, quite another to proclaim that kingdom here, now. And then the most outrageous proclamation of all—God's kingdom includes the poor, the maimed, the blind, and the lame—along with the bigwigs, corporate thieves, and power brokers whom I so despise.

"The kingdom of God has come to you," said Jesus.[46] There was a time when that phrase was rendered into English as, "The kingdom of heaven is *in* you," as if the kingdom was something inward, personal, and private rather than political. While that's an unjustified reading of the kingdom of God, it is true to say that the exchange of citizenship that occurs in the kingdom is also a change of heart. Jesus practiced change of heart as well as change of the world. Much that plagues us originates in the human heart. You can't really hear, "You are a citizen of God's kingdom," and remain the same. Repentance, *metanoia*, is about the world and about the heart. And whenever that happens, the kingdom of God is among you.

Aside to Jesus: O.K., I'll admit it. One of the most difficult aspects of being a Christian is putting up with all these losers and lowlifes you've invited to your party. I like you, but not all of your friends.

A fine young man came to Jesus, claiming that he easily obeyed every single commandment of God since childhood, and asked Jesus what more he should do to be sure he is right with God. Jesus brushed him off, telling him to sell everything he had, every cent, give it up for the poor, and "then come, follow me."[47] With that, the young man got depressed and went away "grieving," because he had lots of stuff. One might have thought that Jesus would have been impressed with the young man's admirable piety. No, Mark says that Jesus "looking at him loved him"[48] and demanded that he sell off everything and follow the way of the Servant. In other words, sell out, sign up, and become part of the kingdom.

The story is noteworthy as (1) the only time Jesus is ever reported to have openly loved a particular person, (2) the only time that we are told explicitly that the recipient of Jesus' invitation was a young adult, and (3) the only time Jesus invited anyone to come into his kingdom as a disciple, yet the person refused. Let those of us in the affluent West take note: the reason for the refusal of the kingdom was material possession.

Matthew says that, when Jesus met Satan in the wilderness at the beginning of his ministry, Satan, after making a few tempting offers, gave up trying to seduce Jesus until a more "opportune time."[49] Satan got nowhere with his taunt, "If you are the Son of God . . ."

That's about all we hear of Satan in the gospels until the end, at the crucifixion. There, the crowd yelled, "If you are the Son of God, throw yourself down from the cross, command God's angels to come save you, if you are truly like God."[50]

See what has happened? Satan isn't there at the cross to make things tough for Jesus because Satan's words ("If you are the Son of God, then . . .") are now on the lips of the crowd. Satan's role as tempter and tormentor has been taken by the crowd, by us. And now, at the cross, Jesus doesn't answer with a loud, "Get out of here, Satan!" Rather, he dies in suffering agony, forgiving his tormentors, stretching out his arms to them in an embrace, Jesus was the God we thought we didn't want, not the God we demanded him to be.

Satan tempted Jesus in the wilderness by offering him all the kingdoms of the world, if only Jesus would worship the world's satanic idea of politics. Satan probably lacked the imagination, as do we, to see that this young adult, alone in the desert, is the world's true King. The young King on the cross now goes forth to claim a kingdom, though many, like Satan, missed it. It's a kingdom of nobodies, ruled over by the King who had no army, no palace, nothing backing up his reign, nothing and no one—except God.

YOU CAN LOOK IT UP

1. *"be no end."* Luke 1:32b-33.

2. *into the wilderness.* Matthew 4:1-11, Luke 4:1-14.

3. *in the wilderness?* Exodus 16:31.

4. *with "wild beasts."* Mark 1:13.

5. *of the sea.* Isaiah 11:1-9.

6. *called it "good,"* Genesis 1:4-31.

7. *hour of salvation!* Luke 4:16 ff.

8. *now, here!* Matthew 13:44 ff.

9. *Wake up!* Luke 16:1 ff.

10. *Jesus warned.* Luke 12:35.

11. *kingdom is now.* Matthew 4:17.

12. *the night shift.* Luke 2:8-20.

13. *the new "king."* Matthew 2:1-15.

14. *"in its branches."* Luke 13:18-19.

15. *"not hear it,"* Luke 10:23-24.

16. *"is among you,"* Luke 17:20-21.

17. *and the foolish.* Luke 14:13.

18. *"not know how."* Mark 4:26-28.

19. *to the Law.* Matthew 23:13.

20. *"triumphing over them."* Colossians 2:12, 15.

21. *"in the age to come."* Ephesians 1:20-21.

22. *"come with power."* Mark 9:1; Matthew 16:28; Luke 9:27.

23. *come back soon.* 2 Peter 3:8.

24. *"only the Father."* Mark 13:32.

25. *of the world.* Matthew 11:20-24; Luke 13:1-5.

26. *"you will laugh."* Luke 6:20-21.

27. *"Your kingdom come!"* Matthew 6:10; Luke 11:2.

28. *"ever and ever!"* Revelation 11:15.

29. *"commit my spirit."* Luke 23:46.

30. *"It is finished."* John 19:30.

31. *kingdom of God.* Luke 22:18.

32. *Christ with them.* Luke 24:45.

33. *a blind man.* John 9.

34. *"in a corner."* Acts 26:26.

35. *"say to you."* Matthew 5:21, 27, 33.

36. *at someone lustfully.* Matthew 5:28.

37. *better or worse.* Matthew 19:8.

38. *better righteousness* Matthew 5:20.

39. *"Christ is Lord!"* 2 Corinthians 4:5.

40. *"taught his disciples,"* Luke 11:1-4.

41. *"our debtors."* Matthew 6:12.

42. *"for his children."* Psalm 103:13.

43. *"rogues, [and] adulterers."* Luke 18:11.

44. *with her tears.* Luke 7:38.

45. *"collectors and sinners"* Matthew 11:19.

46. *"you," said Jesus.* Matthew 12:28.

47. *"come, follow me."* Mark 10:21-22.

48. *"loved him."* Mark 10:21.

49. *more "opportune time."* Luke 4:13.

50. *"truly like God."* Matthew 27:40.

CHAPTER TEN

LOVER

When Jesus finally led his disciples into Jerusalem (on the day the church now calls Palm Sunday), many of his followers expected him, at last, to stand up and act like a Messiah, become king, storm the Roman garrison, and set up a grand new "House of David" government. To their surprise, he bypassed city hall and attacked the temple. Why did Jesus not head for the palace, confront Pilate, and do something really useful rather than make such a fuss over a place of worship?

Jesus grabbed a whip and, kicking over their tables and spilling their precious coins across the floor, drove the money changers from the temple. Jesus' cleansing of the temple,[1] charging the money changers with turning the Lord's house into "a den of thieves," seems a severe, unwarranted reaction. After all, the money changers were there as a public service, following Scripture, helping people to buy the requisite animals for the temple's sacrificial rituals. How did Jesus expect people to worship at the temple? It's like expecting a modern preacher to give a sermon without a Powerpoint projector. How are we to be with God without an appropriate ritual vehicle to get to God? Why, Jesus?

The story of Israel could be read as a record of our repeated attempts to get to God. The story begins in darkness, as progenitor Jacob dreams of a ladder let down from heaven to earth, with heavenly messengers taking God's mail back and forth.[2] In the exodus, much of the biblical account of the escape from Egyptian slavery is consumed with minute details about a portable "tent of meeting" that Israel utilized in the desert in order to meet and to be met by God.[3] Those stories find their culmination in the grand temple in Jerusalem, the center of the world, Mount Zion, where God descends to God's people, and heaven and earth traffic with one another. The temple took almost fifty years to build. Its complex of buildings occupied more than thirty acres and was a wonder of the ancient world. Jews

101

everywhere turned toward the temple in prayer, for it was the place of divine-human meeting. When pilgrims trudged up toward Jerusalem for festivals, they weren't just going up to a beautiful place of worship; they were going to heaven.

Isaiah foretold a day when, not just Jews, but all the nations would stream into the temple singing, "Let's go up to Jerusalem, to the temple where we can learn the ways of God and walk with God."[4] Everybody would gather to worship the true God at the temple, a "house of prayer" for all people.[5]

Jesus seemed strangely, severely critical of the temple. When his disciples expressed awe at the temple's grandeur, Jesus quipped that he could tear the whole thing down and rebuild it in three days (exactly the number of days Jesus' body was in the tomb.)[6] In driving the money changers from the temple, in disrupting the temple system, in healing people outside of the temple's rituals, was Jesus thumbing his nose at the temple hierarchy (notorious collaborators with the Romans)?

John's Gospel says that Jesus was setting himself up as the new "temple," the new means of mediation between God and humanity. Jesus argued with a Samaritan woman at the well.[7] When she said, "You Jews say we've got to go to Jerusalem to worship rightly, and we Samaritans say it's at Mount Gerizim," Jesus responded that, one day soon, "true worshipers will worship the Father in spirit and truth." The woman confessed confusion about what all that "spirit and truth" meant. As for the debate over the liturgically correct location for worship, "Oh well, when Messiah gets here, he'll explain it all to us."

Jesus said, "I am he, the one who is speaking to you." Somehow, discussions about where best to worship were being shifted from Mount Zion to Jesus. About four decades after this exchange between Jesus and the Samaritan woman, the majestic temple lay in ruins. The patience of Emperor Titus ran out with these troublesome Jews. Rome had attempted to pacify the Jews by allowing them to have their temple; now the Romans decided that there was no way to keep Jews quiet without reducing their temple to ashes. Christians came to believe that the temple, the meeting place between God and humanity, was now a man from Nazareth.

The instrument for humanity's encounter with God is, oddly enough, a horrible tool for torture—the cross. Some people think of the cross of Christ as our way to get to be with God in heaven when we die. Surprisingly, the gospels portray the cross first as God's way to get heaven to earth, now. When Jesus breathed his last and died on the cross, Luke says that the curtain in the temple—the veil that separated heaven from earth at the high altar, sinful people from righteous God—was mysteriously ripped in two.[8] Who slashed the curtain? It was as if, in one last, dramatic, wrenching act of self-sacrifice, God ripped the veil of separation between earth and heaven. Now, Israel need not gather on the Day of Atonement (the day of "at-one-ment" with God), stand before the temple, give over their sins to the priest, who would pull back the curtain, enter the temple's holiest place, and offer their sins to God. The curtain was ripped asunder. Now, we could get to God ourselves because God had gotten to us. On the cross, Jesus somehow had done something decisive about the distance between us and God.

Thus, gathered with his disciples in the Upper Room, sharing a meal with them, Jesus called the Passover bread his "body," and urged his disciples to feed on him

Aside to Jesus: So why did I endure six years of seminary and graduate school in theology, then spend two years jumping through the hoops leading to ordination, if you are going to dole out your kingdom to anybody? And without going through proper channels? Surely, my clergy credentials count for something!

for the remission of their sins. He passed around a cup of wine, telling them that the wine was now the sacrificial blood, poured out like the blood was dashed upon the altar in the temple.[9] Whereas the temple was where Israel celebrated the Old Covenant, the "Old Testament" between God and Israel:

- now this cup, this bread were signs of the New Covenant, the "New Testament" God was ratifying with the whole world.
- now, in Jesus, people didn't need to perform an ancient ritual act, blood sacrifice, or engagement in some certified spiritual practice as doled out by the priestly experts at the temple.
- now the necessary ladder from heaven to earth and back again, the moveable tent of meeting, the great high altar on Mount Zion, was among us as Jesus.

· now the world need not come to the temple. God's "temple" had, in vagabond lover Jesus Christ, come out to the whole world.

· now the appointed means to enable humanity to get to God and God to get to humanity was provided by God—God's own Son, Jesus. The work that Jesus did on the cross was redemptive, bringing-us-close-to-God work, which he did for all time, for all people.

All that being said, it's still a shock to see God on a cross. It's not what we expected. Can the problems between us and God be so deep that they could have been set right only by God submitting to such evil human violence? Once again, we see that we cannot affirm "God is love" without risk of grave misunderstanding, any more than we can say, "Jesus is both God and human" without nuance of what we mean by both human and divine. The cross signifies that a deep paradox is built into any accurate picture of Jesus, because we don't expect God to go to such lengths to get to us.

The gospels preach this. For instance, the first thirteen chapters of Mark's Gospel show Jesus as the powerful magician, the all-knowing seer, the divine one who casts out demons and commands the wind and waves, "Be still!" Jesus comes across as a human being but with remarkable, divine powers. When Jesus heals a man with paralysis, the religious leaders ask, "Who is this speaking blasphemy? Who is powerful enough to forgive sin except God alone?"[10]

In chapter 13, the mood shifts and Jesus becomes the human, anguished one who is tormented by thoughts of his imminent arrest. In Mark 14, while dining in darkness at the home of Simon the leper (apparently no healthy person would receive Jesus at such a late hour), an unnamed woman showed up and adoringly poured expensive sweet-smelling oil on Jesus. His disciples (feigning concern for the less fortunate) protested, "She should have sold this oil and given the money to the poor." Jesus told them to show compassion for the poor anytime they want, but that night, "She has anointed my body for burial."[11]

The next night, Jesus shared a last meal with his disciples.[12] During the meal, Jesus tells them that, when the going got rough, all of them would scatter. Peter self-righteously protests, "Though these eleven cowards desert you, you can count on me."[13] Before dawn, when challenged by a little serving girl, Peter cursed and three times denied even knowing Jesus.[14]

The night ended with Peter (nicknamed "The Rock," by Jesus) weeping like a baby in the darkness—the first in a long line of Jesus' best friends who would become grave disappointments to their Master.

Jesus then entered the garden of Gethsemane, saw the prospect of his looming execution, sweated like great drops of blood, and prayed to be delivered.[15] "Oh God, I don't want to die!" Is this any way for God to act? It's as if, in these later chapters of Mark, Jesus the God-human One is Jesus the all-too-human One wrestling with God. Remember that our story began in a garden, the garden of Eden, where Adam and Eve were tested and flunked the exam, disobeying and rebelling against who God created us to be.[16] Now, in another garden, Jesus is confronted with a fork in the road. Jesus can be obedient to God's way, and at grave risk, deliver God's love letter to humanity, or he can act like our primal progenitors and safely go his own way. He can stand up to his adversaries and suffer what they have in store for him, or he can cut and run.

Jesus' anguish in the garden is a great mystery in which the gospels enable us to peer into the depths of divine love. Of Jesus, it can be said, "Truly, he is the Son of God," yet he is no robot unflinchingly plodding toward his death on a cross. He truly is flesh and blood. He did not play-act in Gethsemane; he wrestled with his destiny, crying in anguished dereliction. He was ready to play his part in the divine drama of redemption, *and* he asked to be delivered from it. He was obedient to his Father's loving but risky rescue operation for the world *and* anguished that such painful lengths must be traveled in order to reach the human race. Nobody took Jesus' life—in free obedience, he gave it. In short, in his anguish, he is as the church believed him to be, truly God *and* truly human. And in his obedience, in his complete unity with the Father's loving determination to get back the fallen, murderous human race, he is truly God.

Aside to Jesus: You are really diving deep. Sailing past being "an inspiring moral teacher," you have plunged right to the mysterious depth of the heart of God. Some of the folks reading this book thought that this story was going to help them live a more "purpose-driven" life. Apparently, you intend to go deeper, much deeper.

It takes an expansive, generous mind (such as the one I'm sure God gave you) to wrap itself around so complex a definition of divine love, so rich and mysterious an idea of God. The church would have loved to have presented the world with a simpler God than the Trinity—Father, Son, and Holy Spirit; three distinctive ways of being God, yet truly one God—but there was no way to do that and be faithful to the mystery being worked out in Gethsemane and Calvary.

"Not what I want, but what you want," Jesus says to the Father. Or as the Letter to the Hebrews puts it, "Although he was a Son, he learned obedience through what he suffered."[17] When Jesus cried out, "I don't want to die," he, one with the Father, became a conversation deep within the heart of God. Jesus showed the peculiar nature of God's love: God's love is not sentimental or sweet; it is costly love that is free to love completely, even unto death. Jesus in Gethsemane also embodied God's freedom: God is free to walk away from the horrors of humanity or to love even down to the dregs of suffering and death. In love, God chooses to love all the way to the end.

Still, from what we've seen of Jesus, it's hard to imagine him doing anything less than drinking the cup of suffering down to the bottom and being completely obedient to the Father, for in so doing, Jesus is being true to his deepest self. The God whom Jesus reveals in Gethsemane is not being less-than-godly in this anguish in the garden but rather is disclosing true divinity—suffering, sacrificial love all the way to the end. And the God who loves humanity enough to die with and for humanity revealed what true humanity really is—obedient, trusting love. Here is a God who is only truly known in Gethsemane as the cross looms before him. So when, after the garden, the next day, as Jesus breathed his last and the soldier said, "Truly, this man was the Son of God!"[18] we heard a statement that could be made only at the foot of the cross after a night like that; Jesus is fully human and fully God. God is truly human, and humanity is truly caught up into the divine heart. Mount Calvary has become Mount Zion, with the veil in the temple ripped in two.

A wonder as great as his resurrection was his death on the cross. The miracles he performed were wonderful, but they were temporary fixes to hold death at bay for just a while. Jesus did more than love the world through an occasional good deed here and there—a random act of kindness to somebody's mother-in-law, the restoration of sight to one blind man. On the cross, he accomplished something cosmic and decisive, something that went right to the heart of the matter.

By the way, where were Jesus' disciples during all of his sweat, tears, and anguish in the garden? Once again, true to form, they were sleeping like babes, thereby aggravating Jesus to no end. It isn't like he asked them to die for him; all he asked was that they watch and stay half awake for one hour while he prayed.[19]

Repeatedly, Jesus predicted his death, but his disciples found it impossible to believe.[20] (Are you shocked, having now been introduced to some of the things Jesus said and did, that there were those who still found it hard to believe that things would end badly for Jesus?) Perhaps having seen so much good and so much God in Jesus, it was inconceivable to them that the world eventually would turn on the God who had so graciously, in Jesus, turned to us. Perhaps they just couldn't conceive of anyone named "God" acting in such a way as to get crucified.

So when soldiers came to arrest Jesus, his lead disciple, Peter, swung into action, took matters in hand, drew a sword (Jesus had earlier expressly commanded his people not to take extra baggage while walking with him),[21] and nicked a piece of an ear of the high priest's servant. Jesus rebuked Peter telling him to put away the sword, not because Peter was such a lousy swordsman but because this wasn't at all the way God's reign was meant to come.

"Do you think," Jesus asked, "that I cannot appeal to my Father, and he will at once send me more than twelve legions of angels?"[22]

But that would have been the way of Caesar, not Jesus. Rome promised their allies and subjects peace, security, good highways, and the best legal system in the world. But at a price: high taxes, an oppressive bureaucracy, a far flung military, a few worship services to honor the emperor, and widespread crucifixion of Jews.

Jesus went to the cross between vacillating but dangerous Pilate and the colluding religious authorities. Rome had an economic and military stranglehold upon the whole known world; Jesus commanded his followers never to take up the sword. Jesus' sovereignty was different from Rome's,[23] as is dramatized by the Romans' mockery of Jesus by putting a royal robe upon him and shouting, "Hail king!" just before crucifying him.[24] Rome solidified power with the whip, nails, and cross; Jesus accomplished what he wanted to do through nonviolent, suffering love.

To the mob crying "Crucify him!" Pilate said, "Behold the man," not realizing his double entendre. With his dithering appeasement of the crowd, Pilate proved himself to be anything but a real man. The bedraggled, whipped rabbi before whom Pilate smirked was the real man, the true model for humanity. Yet Pilate was not alone in infamy. Pilate told the chief priests that he was inclined to release Jesus, for this little rabbi was no real threat to the empire.

And the reply of the religious authorities? "If you let Jesus go, you are not really a true friend of Caesar,"[25] they said, implying that they were Caesar's friends. They sealed their apostasy with the astounding claim, "We have no king but Caesar." They, thus, forsook the teaching of the whole Old Testament. How many times did the God of Israel need to say, "I am the one, the only Lord. All the world is mine. I am King"? The cross is a sad reminder to religious leaders of any age about the cost of subservience to the government and the predominate order, the substitution of Caesar's way for that of Jesus.

In Gethsemane and on Calvary's hill, Jesus redefined the sovereignty of God. The One we expected to be the royal victor became the tortured victim. The One who looked like the failed victim became the divine victory. As Paul said, Christ "humbled himself. . . . Therefore God has highly exalted him . . . that, at the name of Jesus, every knee should bow and every tongue confess that Jesus Christ is Lord."[26] The King who reigns from a cross redefines power for the Caesars of all time, be they democratically elected or not. Early Christian preachers, like Matthew, Mark, Luke, and John, told the story of Jesus in such a way that subverts the stories of Augustus, Louis XIV, Queen Victoria, and all the imitators of Caesar closer to home. Sovereignty was redefined on a cross.

On the way to Jerusalem (and in a sense, Jesus was always on his way there, in other words, the way to his death), James and John asked, "Rabbi, do for us whatever we ask."[27]

"Ask," said Jesus.

> Aside to Jesus: You'd better be careful here. Many folks who think they know you believe that all you came to do was to die for their sins and take them to heaven. Your politics is going to make them nervous.

"Let one of us sit at your right and the other at your left when you come into your glory." When you are crowned King, made Messiah, as we know you surely will be, let us sit on your cabinet, sharing in your glory.

Their request must have discouraged Jesus. Here were those who had witnessed his servant leadership, who had shared in his trials, still thinking about power and glory.

"You don't know what you are asking," replied Jesus, "Can you drink the cup I drink or be baptized with the baptism I am baptized with?" He was, of course, talking about his imminent death.

"We can!" they answered. The folly of Jesus' dearest friends is almost boundless.

Then, Jesus responded, "You will drink the cup I drink and be baptized with the baptism I am baptized with, but to sit at my right or left is not for me to grant."

Surely he spoke with irony. In the end, when he was lifted up high on a cross, his disciples where nowhere in sight. On his right and his left were two common criminals.

Hearing about this attempt at one-upmanship by James and John, the other disciples were indignant. Jesus gave them a lesson in leadership, Jesus' style, telling them that they were behaving no better than a bunch of pagans, which must have deeply stung these Jews.

"Whoever wants to become great among you must be your servant; whoever wants to be first must be slave of all," he told them. "For the Son of Man did not come to be served, but to serve, and to give his life as a ransom for many." Jesus died on a cross not to appease the anger and blood lust of God the Father (as the church has sometimes implied) but rather because of the anger and blood lust that the Father's love received from a humanity who wanted nothing so much as to be gods unto ourselves. The cross, which the world erected to silence another uppity Jew, became, in the hands of God, the means whereby God got to us.

Everything about Jesus is cruciform, shaped like a cross. The cross was not just an unfortunate event on a Friday afternoon at the garbage dump outside Jerusalem; it was the way the world welcomed lover Jesus from day one and still does today. Herod tried to kill him when he was yet a wee one in swaddling.[28] From his very first sermon at Nazareth, the world was attempting to summon up the courage to render its final verdict upon Jesus' loving reach, "Crucify him!"

Gethsemane and Calvary bring to a head just about anything I've told you thus far about Jesus. It was not just that Jesus was born in a stable, had compassion for many hurting people, told some unforgettable stories, and taught noble ideals. Rather, the significant thing is that Jesus willingly accepted the destiny toward which his actions drove him, willingly endured the world's response to its salvation. Arrested as enemy of Caesar, and tortured to death as a criminal, Jesus was more than just one more victim of governmental injustice. He was not just an example that good sometimes can come from bad. Rather, as Paul puts it, on the cross, Jesus was victor: Jesus "disarmed the rulers and authorities and made a public example of them, triumphing over them" on the cross.[29] And he did it for Love: the cross is not what God demands of Jesus for our sin but rather what Jesus got for bringing the love of God so close to sinners like us. This is all validated by God raising this crucified victim from the dead, not by dramatically rescuing Jesus' failed messianic project, nor certifying that Jesus had, at last, paid the divine price for our sin. Rather, it showed the world who God really is and how God gets what God wants.

YOU CAN LOOK IT UP

1. *of the temple.* Mark 11.
2. *back and forth.* Genesis 28:12.
3. *met by God.* Exodus 27:21; 33:7.
4. *"walk with God."* Isaiah 2:2-3, paraphrased.
5. *all people.* Matthew 21:13.
6. *in the tomb.* Luke 18:33.
7. *at the well.* John 4.
8. *ripped in two.* Luke 23:35.
9. *altar in the temple.* Leviticus 17:11.
10. *"God alone?"* Mark 2:7, paraphrased.
11. *"for burial."* Mark 14:3-9.
12. *with his disciples.* Mark 14:17-31.
13. *"you can count on me."* Mark 14:26-31, paraphrased.
14. *even knowing Jesus.* Mark 14:66-72.
15. *to be delivered.* Mark 14:32-42.
16. *us to be.* Genesis 1:26-2:25.
17. *"he suffered."* Hebrews 5:8.
18. *"Son of God!"* Mark 15:39.
19. *while he prayed.* Mark 14:32 ff.
20. *impossible to believe.* Matthew 20:18.
21. *walking with him.* Luke 10:4.
22. *"legions of angels?"* Matthew 26:53-54.
23. *different from Rome's.* John 18:13-40.
24. *before crucifying him.* John 19.
25. *"friend of Caesar,"* John 19:12, paraphrased.
26. *"Christ is Lord."* Philippians 2.
27. *"we ask."* Mark 10:35-45, paraphrased.
28. *in swaddling.* Matthew 2.
29. *on the cross.* Colossians 2:15.

CHAPTER ELEVEN

DELEGATOR

No sooner had The Way (the first name for the church)[1] got going than the keepers of the status quo tried to stamp it out. And who can blame them? It was one thing for Jesus to say and do wild things, but it was another to have these "uneducated and ordinary men" (one of the first official verdicts on the church).[2] saying that Jesus had been raised from the dead and had authorized them to say and do the same things as Jesus. They gladly would die rather than recant what they knew to be true: crucified Jesus had been raised from the dead. Such fanaticism and unbalanced devotion! Something had to be done about it.

Which brings us to the drama of Paul.

Scene One: The leader of the make-the-world-safe-for-God movement that was murdering and torturing Christ-followers was a biblically learned "Pharisee among Pharisees," morally righteous man by the name of Saul.[3]

Saul, Church Enemy Number One was on his way from Jerusalem armed with letters from officials and ready to take his stop-Jesus campaign to Damascus. On the way, a blinding light from above struck him down in his tracks. A voice addressed him: "Saul, Saul, why do you persecute me?"

> Aside to Jesus: Why is it that the most violent, well-organized persecutors often know the most Scripture?

In terror, Saul asked, "Who are you?"

"I am Jesus," said the voice. Saul, who had made others victims of his violence, was now a victim. The once cocksure Saul was rendered instantly helpless. He couldn't eat or speak and had to be led around by the hand.

Scene Two: The heavenly voice then went to a follower of Jesus named Ananias, "Go to Straight Street and greet Saul. Welcome him into the church. I've got plans for him to take my way to the pagans."

Ananias responded, "Lord, is this the same Saul who's been ravaging the church?"

"Go!" says the voice. Ananias did as he was told, encountered Saul on Straight Street, addressed him as "brother," baptized him, renamed him "Paul," fed him, and thus assisted in making the greatest missionary and theologian of the early church.

Notice what happened here. The Jesus story didn't end at his crucifixion. It continued, but when the earthly Jesus became the risen Christ, a cast of unlikely characters was enlisted to continue the drama. People like Saul and Ananias were summoned forth to enact the Jesus story. The risen Christ stood in the wings, coaching, calling them when their time came to act their parts, giving them the lines they were to speak. Ordinary people were now acting like Jesus.

The church has sometimes spoken of this story of Saul on the Damascus Road as Paul's "conversion." It certainly is a dramatic turnaround for Saul, so dramatic that he is given a new name. Saul becomes Paul, and church enemy number one becomes the great evangelist of the Gentiles. But it is probably more accurate to call this Paul's "call" rather than his "conversion." Saul already was a Jew, a very devout Jew at that. He wasn't looking for something better in his life. He wasn't searching for a more adequate religion. This isn't a story about that.

It's a story about someone going along with his life, minding his own business (and God's too), only to be blindsided, struck down, called, commissioned, and sent out to do Jesus' business. For some reason known only to the risen Christ, Paul has been chosen for a job. This is the story of world history ever since Jesus—ordinary people are divinely enlisted to what Jesus wants done in the world.

Paul is called by Christ, who first called Ananias to move from regarding Paul as an enemy to welcoming him as a brother. Both Ananias and Paul had their lives turned upside down by vocation, sent places they didn't really want to go, made speeches written by someone else.

Scene Three: A short time later, there is Paul, once a persecutor of Jesus' friends, now speaking up for Jesus in Damascus.[4] "I've been met by the Son of God," preached Paul. The response to Paul's first sermon? The congregation wanted to kill him. In order for Paul to escape death, some of his friends hustle him out of town in a basket. (Remind you of Luke's account of Jesus' first sermon in his hometown?)[5] What they did to Jesus they do to Jesus' friends.

Back when the voice called Ananias to help call Paul, the voice said not only, "He is my chosen instrument to take my name before the pagans," but also, "I will show him how much he must suffer because of me." Saul thought he knew suffering. But then he was met by Jesus, and he really suffered! People who are called by Jesus, converted, and born again are usually summoned not to an easier life but to a life that's more difficult, because they are now working for Jesus.

I'm betting this could be your story too. As you journey toward Damascus, Des Moines, or Daytona, keep looking over your shoulder.

Now, you are unsurprised to see, in all the gospels, the Son of God begin his work in the world by calling a group of twelve ordinary people to drop what they were doing and do what he wanted them to do. Something about Jesus made him choose, from the first, not to save the world by himself. He wouldn't be God alone. Seemingly uninterested in the experience, character, gifts, and skills of his disciples, something propelled the risen Christ toward losers and knuckleheads. As Paul says, perhaps thinking of his own vocation on the Damascus Road, Christ chose what is trash, what is foolish and worthless, to confound the world. He chose them not because they were open and receptive to his teaching, not because he enjoyed hanging out with them, but because he wanted to lay an assignment on them. He lovingly invited them to, "Come unto me" so he could imperiously order them, "Go into all the world!" Almost never did he invite them to settle in, settle down, and find peace and balance; everything was subordinated to the mission. Mark says that he chose the Twelve, "that they might be with him and that he might send them out to preach."[6]

Most of the gospels begin with Jesus walking along a road, seeing some fishermen, and calling out, "Follow me!" They drop their nets and stumble after him. The gospels tell us nothing about the inner feelings, doubts, questions, or beliefs in the hearts and minds of the first disciples. All of the action is outside them. All of this is at Jesus' initiative. The story of the calling of the disciples is not about who they are but who they became once they met Jesus, once he enlisted them in his work.

It was as if Jesus was so confident in his sovereignty that he could afford not to be a micromanager or hands-on leader. He is the quintessential delegator.

Jesus enlists ordinary folks to a much larger project than their own lives. He sweeps us up into a pageant otherwise known as the kingdom of God. Without this summons, this address, our lives are bound to seem small and inconsequential—which Christians believe our lives would be without Jesus. He makes our lives mean more than they could have meant on their own.

"Why Jesus?" To answer, I've tried to resist the temptation to succumb to good old American pragmatic utilitarianism that responds to "Why Jesus?" with "Because Jesus is good for you. Because Jesus is another useful technique to obtain whatever you want in life—peace, adventure, love, security, sexual fulfillment, or whatever it is that you think you've got to have in order to keep going in an often drab world." Or, "Why Jesus? Because Jesus works. You've tried drugs, or a 12-step recovery program, or Eastern spirituality. Now, try Jesus."

That utilitarian, narcissistic approach to Jesus betrays a fundamental misunderstanding of Jesus. Why Jesus? Because Jesus is not here to get what you want out of God; Jesus is God's means of getting what God wants out of you. Jesus is not an effective way whereby we climb up to God; Jesus is God's self-appointed means of getting down to us. Jesus is God Almighty specific, definite, and standing next to you—a frightening thought for modern folks who prefer a God more vague than Jesus the Christ. Really now, if you were dreaming up a useful god to fulfill your every wish and run your every errand, would you have dreamed up Jesus? No way.

Perhaps that's why few people came to Jesus; he went to them. Jesus rarely said, "Love me," and never said, "Agree with me." Rather, he most frequently commanded simply, "Follow me." And not too long after he said "follow me," as soon as we got to know him, he said, "Don't be afraid." What does that tell you about the way he invites us to walk?

It's a fearful thing for someone like Paul, Ananias, me, or you to be called by Jesus, not only because Jesus is often demanding and difficult but also because he places such great faith in his followers. To follow him is to serve him, and to serve him is to be sent out to do what he does: your routine healing, preaching, exorcism, raising hell with the proud and powerful, and raising the dead—that sort of thing.

When you look at the job description for disciples of Jesus, you can understand why hardly anyone came to Jesus; he came to them. Jesus didn't wait for people to feel the need for something better in their lives; he intruded into their lives, turning them upside down. If you are reading in the hope that this book will help you theologically to climb up to Jesus or historically to think back toward him or intellectually to go forward to him, forget it. It's an axiom of Christian theology that our efforts to get to God invariably lead to just another idol, a "god" of our own sweet concoction, the "god" we thought we deserved rather than the God we actually have, a "god" who is easier on us than the one who looks at you and, despite all your faults, says "follow me."

As someone who has worked with Jesus for a long time, I can testify to the benefit of being able to answer, "Why are you a Christian?" with, "Because Jesus called me." To be a Christian is to be someone put here by the great delegator. If the world doesn't like the idea of your being a follower of Jesus, a Christ-bearer into the world, you can say, "Take it up with Jesus. This whole thing was his idea. I tried to beg out of his assignment, but you know Jesus; he won't take 'no' for an answer."

To be a Jesus-follower is more than something that you chose or you decided for yourself (the conventional way that modern people think we are leading our lives). If you follow Jesus down his narrow way, it's primarily because he invited you to walk with him. You got adopted. You got called. As Jesus told his disciples, "You didn't choose me; I chose you that you should go bear fruit in my name."[7]

To us has been delegated the work of the kingdom. Even as he assigns to us his work, surely, he knows that he is calling us to fill roles too big for us. Toward the end of Matthew's Gospel, Jesus offers his parable of the great judgment.[8] (One of his nastiest little stories as far as we religious cognoscenti are concerned.) At the end, the Son of Man shall ascend the throne and judge all the *ethnoi*, all the peoples. On his left will go the goats—who have not done good to the "least of these," have not recognized the incognito Christ among the poor, the imprisoned, and the oppressed—and will be punished. "I was in jail, and you never visited me."

Aside to Jesus: What kind of king gets thrown into jail? And what kind of incarcerated king wants you to visit him there?

On the king's right, will be the sheep, those who having reached out to the "least of these" through their giving, visiting the prisoners, and clothing of the poor, and will be eternally rewarded. "I got busted, and you visited me in jail! Come right into the kingdom."

Here's the shock. In Jesus' story, the sheep talk exactly like the goats— same words, same reaction to the judgment of the Son of Man. "Lord, when did we see you?" The sheep and the goats are equally uninformed.

One expects the goats to be stupid. They don't go to Sunday school, don't use gender-inclusive pronouns for God, don't volunteer for Habitat for Humanity.

But in Jesus' story, *the sheep are as dumb as the goats!* "Lord, when did we see you?"

The blessed sheep knew enough to visit the prisoner or to give the cup of cold water, but they don't see Jesus much more clearly than the unethical, apathetic goats. They're all stupid! When it comes to seeing Jesus, in the end, the sheep are as inept as the goats. Both have nothing more to say for themselves as they stand before the throne of judgment than the dumb: "Lord, when did we see you?"

Jesus' story of judgment is more than a peek at ethically correct behavior; it's the conclusion of a symphony of ignorance. If you thought that Jesus waited for twenty-five chapters of Matthew's Gospel before finally, at the end, giving us sheep the inside scoop, forget it. The disciples—who have had such difficulty figuring out Jesus for twenty-four chapters—are just as stupid at the end as at the beginning. Having followed Jesus since chapter four, they go from dumb to even dumber.

See? We're all amateurs in regard to Jesus. He eludes our grasp, just as he wouldn't be held down at the tomb by Mary Magdalene. There is no way to commandeer or to manage the sovereign judgments of a righteous God. We delude ourselves into thinking that there is some way to be "in the know," to be politically progressive enough, to do all the right things, to ensure that we are on the right side. Then, we can bypass God's judgment because we so knowledgeably see Jesus. No. Jesus loves to shock and surprise the very people who thought they knew him so well. We don't know what we're doing.

But we have faith that Jesus knows what he's doing. Yes, Jesus probably should have called and chosen someone else to "go and bear fruit." Yes, you've got your limitations. Yet, by God's grace and the stories and actions of Jesus, we know what God is doing. Believe that God knows what God is doing by calling someone like you to witness to the kingdom. Sure, the shoes are too big for you. Sure, you have doubts, fears, and big reservations.

Jesus can work with all that; he has done so ever since the calling of the first disciples. The composition of the citizenry of the kingdom is the prerogative of the King. Salvation belongs not to any of us but to "the Lamb,"[9] to the one who sits on the throne. The guest list is God's and God has done everything necessary ("It is finished") for us to join the party, and God invites us all, now, here. Thank God that, though Jesus preaches righteousness, he also loves to forgive sinners, sinners who are either his worst enemies or his closest friends, but all sinners.

Aside to Jesus: I hope you know what you are doing. You sure put a great deal of confidence in the poor old church. Sometimes you have more faith in us than we have in you!

The First Letter of Peter speaks of all Christians, all the baptized, not just the church's leaders or clergy, when it says that everybody in the body of Christ is a preacher, a part of the "royal priesthood," not priests in the church but priests in the whole world: "But you are a chosen race, a royal priesthood, a holy nation, God's own people, in order that you may proclaim the mighty acts of him who called you out of darkness into his marvelous light."[10]

Jesus is the great Delegator, the one who refuses to reign alone, the one who enlists ordinary women and men to work with him and for him, to be his body, commissioned to be the only glimpse of Jesus most people will ever see. Even after hammering one of his churches for all its shortcomings, Paul blurts out, "Now you are the body of Christ and members of it."[11] Jesus, one with God Almighty on high, has taken up residence on earth, has launched the first wave of the invasion, and has touched down firmly in this world, one with his body, his family, the church. You, the church, are the "righteousness of God," said Paul.[12] We are a visible, bodily sign of what God can do, and is doing, in the world to set things right. "God is making his appeal [to the world] through us,"[13] said Paul. We are God's sermon. We are God's loving invitation to the world to "join up," not just joining another human organization but also to be joined with Christ.

Some historians believe that Christianity triumphed because Jesus, God incarnate, gave birth to an organization that astounded the world with its acts of charity in his name. In the first centuries of the Christian era, when at least two plagues decimated the Roman population, and rich people and their priests fled the cities, the Christians stayed and cared for the sufferers, no matter who they were. In just a century or so, this small sect became the dominant faith of the empire. These Christians put into practice a story and an ethic that was a rebuke and an alternative to the ways of the culture. Thus, the world took note of Jesus by noticing his followers. Jesus was first known, and is perhaps still best known, by the quality of lives that he is able to produce through his summons, "Follow me."

Jesus' people are to look and act differently than the world. He works with a countercultural notion of greatness:

> You know that among the Gentiles those whom they recognize as their rulers lord it over them, and their great ones are tyrants over them; but it is not so among you. But whoever wishes to become great among you must be your servant, and whoever wishes to be first among you must be slave of all. For the Son of Man came not to be served but to serve, and to give his life a ransom for many.[14]

Jesus dared to offer himself as the model for his followers. Jesus' people dare to attempt to copy Jesus. Rather than lower the bar to the level where almost anybody could succeed as a disciple, he raised the bar so high that no one could succeed without lots of divine help. Jesus really cranked things up—from adultery meaning having sex with somebody to adultery meaning having lustful desire for somebody, from theft meaning taking somebody's stuff to theft meaning just badly wanting somebody's stuff. It's almost like he set the bar so high that, since Jesus, nobody could say "the point of religion is trying to live a good, moral life." His ethics turned everybody into a scoundrel, even as it promised that everybody could be a saint.

There was a time when Jesus made sense to North American culture, when being a follower of Jesus was the thing to do. That time is over. You are fortunate to be thinking about Jesus in an age when much of the world thinks Jesus is odd, out of place, and nonsensical. As you have seen, Jesus was wary of popularity and public acclaim. Paul called himself, "Christ's fool."[15] Nobody could say what Jesus said or be like he is and expect a warm, popular reception from the folks at home.

After his resurrection, Jesus "presented himself alive to them by many convincing proofs, appearing to them over the course of forty days and speaking about the kingdom of God."[16] Then the very last thing Jesus (always the Delegator) said to them was "you will be my witnesses in Jerusalem, in all Judea and Samaria, and to the ends of the earth."[17]

Three days after his brutal crucifixion, on Sunday, the first day of the Jewish work week, a couple of disciples trudged from Jerusalem to the little village of Emmaus. They were depressed. Jesus, the one in whom they had hoped, had been defeated, now three days sealed in the tomb.

They realize that a stranger had joined them on the road. He talked with them, discussed Scripture with them, and when they arrived at the inn at Emmaus, they invited the stranger to stay with them.

Well, you know the rest: the stranger took the bread, blessed it, broke it, and gave it to them. In an instant, their eyes were opened and they saw that the stranger was none other than Jesus. The Jesus movement into the world hasn't ended; it's begun. They ran all the way back to Jerusalem to tell the others the news.

In a way, this is not only a parable of Sunday morning in church but also a definition of just who a Christian is. A Christian is someone who has been surprised by Jesus. The risen Christ loves surprises. We're just walking along, minding our own business, when suddenly, Jesus shows up, surprises us, joins our table, feeds us, talks to us, opens the Scriptures, and we see, to our amazement, that Jesus has invited himself into our lives. When that happens, brace yourself; there's a good chance he's going to assign you a job.

YOU CAN LOOK IT UP

1. *the church.* Acts 9:2.
2. *verdicts on the church.* Acts 4:13.
3. *the name of Saul.* Acts 9.
4. *in Damascus.* Acts 9:20-25.
5. *in his hometown?* Luke 4:16-30.
6. *"send them out to preach."* Mark 3:13-19.
7. *"in my name."* John 15:16, paraphrased.
8. *the great judgment.* Matthew 25:31-46.
9. *to "the Lamb,"* Revelation 22:1.

10. *"into his marvelous light."* 1 Peter 2:9.
11. *"of it."* 1 Corinthians 12:27.
12. *"God,"* said Paul. 2 Corinthians 5:21.
13. *"through us,"* 2 Corinthians 5:20.
14. *a ransom for many.* Mark 10:42-45.
15. *"Christ's fool."* 2 Corinthians 11:16, 23.
16. *"of God."* Acts 1:3.
17. *"the earth."* Acts 1:8.

CHAPTER TWELVE

BODY

I n Jesus, words took on muscle.[1] There are some people who think of Jesus as "spiritual." Jesus is that vaguely divine something that enables you to pump yourself full of helium and rise above the grubbiness of life in this carnal world. Wrong. The Christian faith, taking its cues from Jesus, is insistently material, corporeal, anthropomorphic, muscular, and incarnational. "The Word became flesh."[2] God's Word has become a person, a person in motion. Jesus is God Almighty daring to get physical; God with a body, a body in action.

Greek philosophy (that is, ancient Greek religion after Plato) is obsessed with how to get over the body. How can we—through philosophical meditation on higher things—rise above this frail, dirty, decaying flesh and into some sweetly disembodied eternity?

Jesus, being a Jew, couldn't care less. Jews don't divide persons into antimonies of spirit versus flesh like the Greeks do. No Jew ever wanted a disembodied life, either now or the next. After his body was brutally crucified, Jesus moved, not out of a body but rather into a body of a very different sort.

So at last we come to maybe the most offensive part of the story—Jesus has a body. I didn't say that Jesus *had* a body. Everybody knows that Jesus slept, ate, wept, and bled and then agonizingly died. What everybody doesn't yet know is that, though the tomb was bare of Jesus' body, Jesus was back—in a resurrected body. He came and went in an instant, unconfined by time and space, passing through doors and appearing at the most awkward moments. But it was nevertheless a body in which Jesus was recognizable to those who had known him before. His after-Easter body enabled him, invited or not, to share a number of meals and arguments with his astonished followers, which became for them irrefutable proof that "Christ was raised from the dead."[3]

When Christians affirm the Creed, "We believe in the resurrection of the body," we're saying that we believe that the same God who raised Jesus from the dead shall somehow, someday raise us, but not as ghosts or disembodied spooks. Paul said that our perishable body will put on an "imperishable" body, whatever that means.[4] The dead shall be raised just as Jesus was raised.[5] "We will all be changed."[6] We'll have spiritual bodies.[7] There's no person without a body and, in saying that we believe that God will raise our dead bodies to new bodies, we are saying that we believe in the resurrection of persons with recognizable personalities. Specifics of that grand resurrection, such as date and form, are still matters of speculation.

Here's something even more remarkable: Paul is convinced that Jesus continues to have a "body," persists in taking up room on this earth, keeps showing up as a specific, recognizable personality, but now in an even stranger corporeal form than his resurrected post-Easter body. Paul's fellow Christians knew Jesus not only as Savior, home wrecker, storyteller, and sovereign but also as lover who, in cross and resurrection, intimately united with his people, a delegator whose followers had been delegated to be his "body." Now, the same Jesus who once walked Galilee shows up all over the world in and through them, showing up not in his previous body but for the very same purposes. Now Jesus is no longer confined even to his remarkably itinerate resurrected body. During his earthly ministry, vagabond though he was, Jesus traveled less than a hundred miles from home. Now, his widely dispersed body races toward "Jerusalem, in all Judea and Samaria, and to the ends of the earth,"[8] so that there's nowhere on earth you can be where Jesus didn't get there before you.

Some sentimental souls think of Jesus as a fine person, a Savior even, but one who never intended to found a church. But there already was "church," from the very beginning of the story of Jesus. Jesus, the great Delegator, didn't just call individuals; he called a group, a body, twelve disciples. The Jesus movement was a corporate, social movement; not a conglomeration of religiously inclined individuals. If you meet Jesus, then you must be introduced to him through the corporate lens of his first followers (Paul and the gospels). Jesus is so embedded in his body, from the very first, that there's no way to extricate some "real Jesus" or "original Jesus" from the Jesus as presented by those who first followed him.

So in the Creed, we say not only that we believe in "Jesus Christ" but also that we believe in "one holy, catholic church." Sometimes it's easier to believe that Jesus is the Son of God than to believe that the church is the Son of God's holy body! Paul says in 1 Corinthians 12: "Just as the body is one and has many members and all the members of the body, though many, are one body, so it is with Christ."[9] Note that Paul is saying more than that the church has lots of different members who all ought to work together. Rather, Paul says that Christ has many diverse parts of his "body," and we are it. And we're all in this together. Though each has his or her own iden-tity and function, we are together as Jesus' body. We are one, not because we are all in agreement or even because we all like each other; we are one body because we've got one Lord who just loves to bring people together. We are like the hands and feet and the mouth and eyes of Christ, the only body God has. If the world is going to meet Jesus, it will need to meet him as his body, the church.

> Aside to Jesus: You sure are easier to live with when you are spiritual than when you get physical.

Paul is being more than merely metaphorical in calling the Christian community Jesus' "body." "I have been crucified with Christ; and it is no longer I who live, but it is Christ who lives in me,"[10] said Paul. Christ is not merely with us but "in us." Jesus did not die and rise just to forgive our sins and give us a future life. He gave us life, not just some day in heaven but here on earth, not just a vague feeling within but new life in the world. Back when Paul encountered the risen Christ on the Damascus Road, the voice from the blinding light cried, "Saul, Saul, why do you persecute me?"[11]

One expects Saul/Paul to reply, "I'm not persecuting you. I'm beating up on these dumb Christians who are violating Scripture." But, no, in the eyes of the risen Christ, you mess with the church, and you attack Christ's very own body.

Jesus says to the world that to receive one of his disciples is to welcome Jesus just as whoever welcomes Jesus welcomes God.[12] Disciples, now dele-gated to be Jesus' body, do most of the things that Jesus does, under his authorization.[13] And the world treats Jesus' disciples in much the same fash-ion as it treated him.[14] Paul said that he carried in his own body "the death of Jesus, so that the life of Jesus may also be made visible in our bodies we are always being given up to death for Jesus' sake, so that the life of Jesus may be made visible in our mortal flesh."[15] What they did to Jesus' body, they do to his disciples' bodies. (Back on the road, when Jesus told us to take up our cross daily, we thought it was merely a metaphor.) In our faithful, embodied following of Jesus, we are Jesus' new presence in the world. Paul even claims, "It is no longer I who live, but it is Christ who lives in me."[16] Christ has taken up residence in Paul's body so that Paul could be Jesus' body in the world. Obviously, in calling the church the "body of Christ," the line between Jesus Christ and the friends of Jesus Christ is being shockingly blurred.

Paul's talk of body makes Jesus more than a helpful moral example or a wise spiritual guru. Jesus Christ is the living God intimately with us, in us. I also hope that you see that the faith engendered by Jesus is much more than, "Now, I know I'll get to go to heaven when I die." Hardly anybody said that about Jesus. Rather, what they said was, in so many words, "Jesus is intimately among us; heaven has come down to earth. Now I know that I'll get to really live before I die. And when I die, I'll die in the confidence that the same Jesus who risked so much to get me in life will do the same in death." Jesus is God's great rescue operation, God's risky reach toward us, and God's loving embrace of us, here, now, so that he may have us forever. Jesus is not how we sail away up to heaven (like all that hooey among some Christians about the "rapture"). Jesus is God coming to us, here, now, heaven come to earth. Jesus doesn't wait to be of relevance to us someday when we die; Jesus makes us fully alive now. The great "temple" where we come close to God is Jesus. "I am bread, feed on me."[17] There's no great, new truth about God awaiting our discovery. In Jesus, God has intimately revealed to us the grand, full truth about God, at least all we can take of the truth. Emmanuel. The curtain is ripped open and we see, we know God With Us.

"I had always heard about love," the sappy, misty-eyed student said to me, "but until she came into my life, I didn't know what love really is. She is so much a part of me that I never again can say 'me.' Now it's all 'us.'" Forgive me this sentimental digression, but it parallels nicely what Paul knows about the body of Christ. (Yes, dear, it's true that the word that's translated as "to know" in the Old Testament can also mean to understand, to comprehend. But in the Bible it can also mean carnal intercourse, to have sex.[18] Now, that's knowledge!)

Elsewhere, the church is even called the "bride" of Christ—the church is Jesus doing with the world in public that which husbands and wives do alone in marriage.[19] Is that enough bodily intimacy for you? Revelation says that the world will be brought to its grand finale when the kingdom comes, God's will is done on earth as in heaven, and there will be a massive "marriage supper of the lamb."[20] This poor, old tart, the church, will, at last, be arrayed in virginal white, at last, the beautiful bride that Christ believes her to be, and the union between God and God's people will be fully consummated.

Even as I say that, I blush. Believe me, I know the church and its weaknesses better than you. In fact, I am one of the church's greatest weaknesses. Christ's body it may be, but it is a crucified body, shot through with gaping wounds, nail holes in its hands and feet. I know people who can readily believe that Jesus lived a great life, made some remarkable statements, was unjustly crucified, and rose from the dead. But show them a church, and they'll never believe that such a ragtag collection of losers could have any connection to what they love about Jesus! Jesus prayed that his disciples would "all be one" so that the world might believe.[21] To this day one of the reasons for disbelief in Jesus is the sad, divided state of Jesus' body.

Oh, the boredom of the church, the irrelevance of its locked doors and smug, self-righteousness! I could go on. Still, as Paul says when looking at the church, though we don't yet see that spotless, virginal bride of Christ, we do see "through a glass, darkly,"[22] "we hope for what we do not yet see,"[23] and the old girl, for all her lurid past, can look fairly good when made up for worship on Sunday or serving soup to the poor on a Monday.

I can be so candid about the flaws in Christ's body, the church, because the Scripture that gives rise to the church, the ancient testimony that constantly comforts the church, also bears within itself the most severe contemporary critique of the church. Jesus' first disciples are often presented as blithering idiots not only because they probably were but also because they caution us contemporary idiots, that the church, in any age, is never completely the church Christ intends the church to be. "Bride of Christ" she may be, but sometimes, she dallies with other suitors. Read a little church history, and you will discover the persistent truth—the church fools around.

And yet, despite the unflattering portraits of the church within Scripture itself, on the basis of Christ's promises in Scripture, as well as our own weekly experience for more than two thousand years, the poor, old church can believe that, for better or worse, this is the form that the risen Christ has chosen in the world. The only one whom God has ever raised from the dead is the same one who said, "I am the good shepherd. The good shepherd lays down his life for the [dumb, wayward, foolish, asinine, promiscuous, lost, and wandering] sheep,"[24] or words to that effect. That's a shepherd with an extravagant notion of animal husbandry. "Here, eat my body, drink my blood. I'm giving it for you," Jesus said to his disciples at the table one evening.[25] That's an extravagant idea of the perfect host.

The church marvels that a bunch of losers like us (as you have seen, from the first, Jesus was never too discriminating in deciding with whom to party) could be that place where earth and heaven meet. Every time the church gathers for a family night supper, a Bible study, a sermon, a pontifical high mass, a house raising for the poor, or a holy-roller meeting we do so under his promise that if just two or three of us manage to show up in his name, he'll be there.[26] We discover, in the gatherings of the poor, old church a truth: God was in Christ, "reconciling the world to himself."[27]

At the end of Luke's and Matthew's Gospels, the risen Christ promises to return (the "second coming" as Christians sometimes speak of his return.)[28] What Christ began shall be finally, completely finished. The whole creation reconciled to God,[29] and the people of God fully redeemed,[30] the marriage with the Lamb will finally be consummated. Jesus will not return just to his exclusive club of followers; rather he will "come and gather the people of all nations and languages and they will come to see God's glory."[31] "All people will see this," all will be welcomed home."[32]

For now, the world is still in process of redemption. The rescue operation continues. Not everything wrong with this life has been set right by Jesus; not everything about the church looks like it is supposed to. The church has yet to open itself to peoples of all nations and languages, to tell the story and to be the story so that all might believe that God really has shown up in Jesus. But by the grace of God, enough is revealed to give us hope. Not every Sunday, but on many, we catch a glimpse of what God promises one day to do forever. Christ shall be "all in all"[33] and what was once only a glance of the kingdom shall be on earth as in heaven, obvious and apparent, forever and ever.

I'm in the business of words and I think the world of words but I doubt that Jesus would have been crucified—I'm sure there would be no church— if all we had were the words of Jesus. From the first, the thing that really attracted some people and disturbed others (usually people in authority)

were not the words of Jesus, it was Jesus himself. Herod tried to extermi-
nate him when he was but a babe, even before he could say, "Abba." He was
God in the flesh, here, now, but not the God we wanted. What attracted the
hapless, helpless, hurting multitudes, what convened the church, was not
the assorted writings about Jesus; it was Jesus. His resurrected presence
("I'm back and I'll never let you go") birthed the church. Not the church's
pumped-up memories of Jesus or sentimental notions about Jesus; it was
Jesus.

Why Jesus? Because abstract, general truth does not stir much among
us. When truth becomes embodied, up close and personal, present truth,
then truth becomes interesting and we know for sure that "the kingdom of
God has come near."[34] Not that Christ is fully contained by the church;
nothing human can do that. It is more true to say that Christ graciously
visits the church, becomes uniquely present to the church, commands and
criticizes most often the church, keeps rescuing and resurrecting the
church, so much so that the church has good reason to call itself his body in
motion.

The truth to which the gospels testify cannot be verified in the dusty
archeology of history or by the complicated ideas of theologians. The truth
is in his presence, Jesus' undeniable nearness in bread and wine, in those
fellow travelers gathered with us about his table, his works of love and mercy
in the world done by his people. For all its faults, one great thing about
being grafted into Jesus' body, the church, is to have your little life swept up
into something larger than your life, a family bigger than the one into
which you were born, an adventure that's more than your life could have
been on its own.

Back to the beginning of this "Why Jesus?" journey: the way Luke tells it,
in the darkness, three days after Jesus' crucifixion, a group of women went
out to Jesus' tomb.[35] They were stunned: The tomb was empty. Two men in
dazzling clothes appeared. The women were terrified. They ran back to
Jerusalem to tell the apostles. The disciples concluded that the women were
nuts.

Lead apostle Peter went to the tomb later in the morning, had a look-see
and was amazed, but none the wiser. Sometime later, when Jesus appeared
to the men, Luke says that they "were startled and terrified and thought they
were seeing a ghost."[36] Note that in all this commotion nobody yet believes
the crucified Jesus has been raised from the dead. The women seem to have

concluded, at first, that someone had stolen the body. The men thought that they had seen a spook. The idea of resurrection occurred to none. Resurrection was something that they neither wished for nor expected.

Only gradually they came to the conviction that Jesus was raised from the dead because the risen Christ returned to them. The empty tomb told the astonished disciples almost nothing. Saint Paul makes much of resurrection appearances but never mentions an empty tomb. Though Luke narrates a story about the empty tomb, he mostly delights in telling how the followers of Jesus enjoyed a full forty days of meals and conversations with the risen Christ before he finally ascended to God the Father. It was not the empty tomb that led to their belief that the crucified Jesus had been raised from the dead. Rather it was Jesus' return to them, his presence with them, his undeniable intimacy with them in bread and wine, in sermons and acts of love and mercy, that led them to fling in the face of the world's objections that the crucified Jesus has been raised from the dead.

About the last thing the risen Christ says to his disciples in the Gospel of Matthew is, "I am with you until the close of the age."[37] Did they take this as a reassuring promise or as a kick-in-the-seat-of-the-pants threat? The same Jesus who had so fiercely driven them for three dangerous years in Galilee and Jerusalem now promised to pursue them "into all the world," hounding them "until the close of the age." That was good news, sort of.

Aside to Jesus: I keep thinking you could have made belief in you easier, more self-evident, with lots of unassailable, uncontestable *facts.* How come you didn't make a knock-down argument for yourself? You seem to have set it all up in such a way that there is so much risk of getting it wrong, so many gaps and unanswered questions, so little certitude—and so great need to trust.

So the poor old church becomes the best "proof" of the resurrection, if you insist on evidence. If you don't believe that Jesus was raised from the dead, then how do you explain the continued presence of his body, the church? How do you account for the unassailable fact that these defeated, depressed disciples, scattered back to their homes after the crucifixion, shaking like frightened rabbits behind locked doors, are shortly thereafter launching an all-out assault upon Caesar's empire with their preaching and teaching, completely overtaking Caesar's vast legions without drawing a sword or engaging in a single battle—unless the testimony of women is true? Our chief proof of the continued presence of Jesus Christ is the continued presence of his church. God is able to produce a new people, "by water and the Spirit"[38] (baptism) who confound the ways of the world, a people whose convening is so against the wisdom of the world that there's no way to explain their existence other than, God has raised crucified Jesus from the dead and he has returned to his followers, commanding them to go into all the world to tell the world the whole truth about God.

Not many of these early preachers said "Jesus is raised, now we'll all get to go to heaven when we die and live forever." Rather, they said Jesus is raised; what Jesus said about God is true. Despite what we thought about his defeat on the cross, God's great new world is breaking in right now, before our very eyes. Now we've got to show and tell the whole world the truth.

As you may have noticed, there are a number of differences in the way Matthew, Mark, Luke, and John tell the story of Easter and its aftermath. What do we make of these divergences? I believe they are testimony to the difficulty of articulating something as inconceivable as Jesus' resurrection. Early Christians were totally unprepared by anything they knew about reality to conceive of a fact so strange as the resurrection of a person from the dead. They therefore struggled, within limited human experience, to talk about an event that shatters accustomed frames of reference and set their world on its head. In short, the differences among the gospels in talking about the resurrection are a testimony to its reality.

Jews did not think much about the idea of resurrection. They had little notion of "life after death." Where the idea of a resurrection crops up, in visionary writings like that of Ezekiel[39] or 2 Maccabees[40] it is associated with the working of God's justice. Resurrection is when God sets right the wrong that has been done to God's family in this world. Furthermore, if there was to be a hoped-for justification of the Jewish victims of pagan injustice, it would be a general resurrection—everybody who had died as victims of injustice would be raised. So much wrong has been done in this life that if God is truly a just and righteous God, then we can hope that God will set things right in the future, some life beyond death. Resurrection was never the idea that it's just not fair for human beings to die (Genesis says up front that everybody comes from dust and returns to it).[41] Rather, the idea of resurrection in Israel developed out of a conviction that God's justice shall one day triumph, even in the face of present injustice and death. So when Jesus' disciples heard the women proclaim, "He is risen from the dead," they really had very little with which to think that through.

In the days shortly thereafter, Jesus' followers came to believe that the raising of Jesus from the dead was a stunning victory of God. God had raised the unjustly tortured and rejected Jew, Jesus, from the dead, so Jesus must have been the full revelation of God despite much of the world's rejection of Jesus. They had no notion of God raising any individual—those Jews who believed in resurrection believed in a general, national resurrection, not the raising of an individual. That Jesus alone was raised proved to them the quite unique identity of Jesus.

Above all, they came to believe that Jesus' resurrection said something definitive about God. In this world, the friends of God may suffer injustice, torture, and even death. Yet you can be sure that God will have the last word. The Gospel of John opens with, "In the beginning was the Word, and the Word was with God, and the Word was God." John is saying that Jesus is God's word to the world. And in the resurrection of Jesus, God has had the last word on our death and our sin. That word is victory, forgiveness, triumph, life.

One explanation of Easter that will not do is the *au courant* academic fantasy that the disciples of Jesus worked themselves into such a frenzy of grief over the death of Jesus that they succumbed to mass hysteria and said, "You know, when we get together it's almost like Jesus is still with us." This is the old he'll-live-on-in-our-memories rationalization of Easter.

Sorry, such an explanation explains nothing. For one thing, we have noted that the main reaction of the disciples to "Jesus is raised" was fear. They didn't expect Jesus to be raised from the dead; in a sense they didn't really want him raised from the dead. For another thing, has anything you have learned thus far about Peter suggested to you that he had a fertile imagination or a creative mind?

Even when, at the end of Matthew's Gospel, the risen Christ appears to his disciples on the mountaintop for a final commissioning, Matthew says that though some of the disciples "saw" and "worshiped him," still "some doubted."[42] Jesus was right there before them, and some holdouts doubted! You see what these early Christian preachers like Matthew are doing? If you have trouble swallowing all this, don't worry; this has always been our reaction to the risen Christ. The gospels are not asserting a knockdown argument for Jesus' resurrection. They are telling the story in an honest way, truthfully admitting their doubts, not providing much evidence for their claims, other than their own cockeyed conviction that it's all true. Nobody was more surprised by Jesus' resurrection than his own disciples and nobody is a surer testimony for Jesus' resurrection than his own disciples, now become the church. The presence of Jesus was not something that they badly wished for; it was an event that scared them half out of their wits. Some got it and some didn't; some worshiped him as resurrected, reigning Lord, and others doubted—almost like your average body of Christ gathering on any Sunday.

By the way, if any of what I'm saying makes sense to you, if you believe there is a good chance that what I'm claiming for Jesus is true, then all that is gift, sure sign of the near presence of Jesus to you. The Holy Spirit is the name for the enabling power, the near presence of the Father and the Son to the church and the world. When most Christians feel the risen Christ to be especially, powerfully, productively present, we often call that action, that distinctive personality of God, "The Holy Spirit." The Holy Spirit teaches, explains, empowers, prods, and encourages. Paul says it's our "guarantee," our "down payment" of what's to come, a taste of the glory yet to be revealed.[43]

To talk of one "person" of the Trinity is to talk about all three who just happen to be one. You can't say anything definitive about Jesus, such as "Jesus is loving," that doesn't apply to God the Father and God the Holy Spirit. You can't say anything about God the Holy Spirit, such as "the Holy Spirit is powerful and creative," that doesn't apply to God the Father and God the Son. You can't say anything about God the Father, such as "God is righteous and watchful," that doesn't apply also to God the Holy Spirit and God the Son. The Holy Spirit is the spirit of Jesus in action, and Christ the Son gives content and specificity to the mysterious, energetic Holy Spirit.

Jesus told his disciples that when the authorities haul you into a courtroom (note that he doesn't say "if" they arrest you and throw you in the slammer), don't plan your defense speeches to the court in advance: "When they bring you before the synagogues and the rulers and the authorities, do not be anxious how or what you are to answer or what you are to say; for the Holy Spirit will teach you in that very hour what you ought to say."[44]

That's why, when Scripture is read or a sermon is preached, we often pray, "Lord Jesus, open our hearts and minds by the power of your Holy Spirit so that we can hear what you want to say to us today," or words to that effect. The Holy Spirit is a great teacher, telling us things we could never come up with on our own. Just as Jesus preached "in the power of the Holy Spirit" in Nazareth,[45] so Jesus' Holy Spirit enables us to speak about Jesus and to hear Jesus. Even faith in Jesus is a gift of Jesus in the power of the Spirit. As Paul put it, "No one can say 'Jesus is Lord,' except by the Holy Spirit."[46]

While I hope that my introduction of friend Jesus might make it easier for you to "believe in Jesus and believing him might have eternal life,"[47] it might not. For one thing, I've admitted the belief that Jesus is as much of God as we ever hope to see. Belief is a gift, grace. Faith that Jesus really is who he says he is, and who the witnesses in the New Testament say he is, and who I say he is, is not a matter of clear thinking or earnest effort—faith is a gift of God. God's salvation of the world, God's restoration of all things to God, God's forgiveness of our sin is always something that God does. It's miracle, all the way down. If my awkward, dead words rise up off this page, grab you by the scruff of the neck, and shake you, it's a miracle somewhat like Jesus' raising of Lazarus.

Aside to Jesus: As an author, could I just say that one challenge in talking about you is your tendency to take over a text, to commandeer my words, and to make them say more than I intended? See? I'm losing control over the book I thought I was writing.

Jesus sometimes doesn't make sense, as the world makes sense, because Jesus can be difficult and demanding: "Deny yourself! Take up your cross! Follow me!" So it's hard to say that you love Jesus or that you believe in Jesus without obeying Jesus. And if you obey Jesus, as he clearly expects us to do, you will be changed by Jesus. There is a cost of discipleship. Because this is a book about Jesus, this book could be more expensive than what you paid for it. Jesus changes just about everybody whom he loves, especially those who attempt to love him in return. Sometimes people (like me) write books about Jesus, and sometimes people (like you) read books about Jesus as an unconscious means of avoiding following Jesus.

Still, beware. You have reason to be nervous. Jesus is good at getting what he wants, and the full testimony of Scripture contends that Jesus wants *you*.

When it comes to Jesus, your feelings and your thinking may not be the heart of the matter anyway. John the Baptizer was quite specific about how people ought to respond to his preaching about the arrival of the kingdom, how they were to get ready to greet the Christ: if you have too many clothes, clothe those who don't. Stop hoarding food; share. Soldiers, stop using force to rob.[48] Note that John doesn't mention anything about a change of heart or shift in feelings. (Nor does he mention the need to read a book about it!)

Most of us find it impossible to follow Jesus without staying close to Jesus' body, the church, because Jesus is just too demanding and difficult to go it alone. We need help from our friends who know how rough the ride can be when you are journeying with Jesus. Church is not only where Jesus becomes embodied but also where our faith in Jesus gets fleshed out too. Church is where ordinary people are not only enabled to hear the invitation, "Follow me," but also where we are able to obey the command, "Follow me."

Still, despite our failures, Jesus keeps saying, "Follow me." He keeps betting on losers, keeps loving sinners, keeps treating us as if we could be saints, as if we were good enough to die for. If Jesus can love you adulterers, murderers, tax collectors, and whores, I'm counting on him also mustering some affection for preachers and writers of books about him— although I'm sure that Jesus desires disciples who obey him more than he longs for writers and readers who think about him. The truth of Jesus is not proven by admiring him, but rather by following him, by offering our lives to him in his service, by having the guts to journey, to step forward at his invitation, "Follow me."

One of Jesus' nasty little stories involves two brothers whose Dad said to them, "Please pitch in and help with some of the work in the field."[49]

One of the brothers said, "Drop dead, Dad" (didn't we meet this guy in an earlier Jesus story?), and settled back on the couch to watch his favorite program. Shortly thereafter, the father looked up and saw this smart-mouthed son bent down, hard at work in the turnip patch.

The second brother said, "Yes, Father dear, I'd be delighted to do what I can to help the family business." Two days latter, this seemingly docile lad was still hanging around the house, fooling with his computer, hands unsullied with manual labor.

"Now think hard," says Jesus, "which of the two brothers pleased his father?" You don't have to have a Ph. D. in theology to know the answer. (However it might help to have a Ph. D. to figure out why Jesus concludes this parable with "John the Baptist warned you but nobody but tax collectors and whores believed him!")

"Not everybody who uses the right words, crying 'Lord!' 'Lord!' gets my ear," said Jesus. "But everyone who does my will."[50] Often Jesus asked his critics, "Have you not read?" referring them to some passage from the Hebrew Scriptures.[51] Of course they had read the Bible. But with Jesus, simply reading Scripture wasn't enough. Something else was required—discipleship. Jesus is best known by obeying Jesus, by putting down the book and following Jesus. In trying to act like Jesus, we come to know Jesus. "Follow me," often precedes "Know me."

Despite the misguided efforts of many, the darkness has not quenched the light. The good news has never been silenced. Jesus yet speaks. We don't have to struggle to find Jesus; he finds us. In every age, to a few adventurous souls, he whispers, sometimes shouts: "Come! Peek behind the veil, turn, become as a little child, take up the cross, pass the bread, share the wine, get born again, join the journey. Be dangerous. Let the party begin."

YOU CAN LOOK IT UP

1. *took on muscle.* John 1:1-14.
2. *"Word became flesh."* John 1:14.
3. *"from the dead."* Romans 6:4.
4. *whatever that means.* I Corinthians 15:51.
5. *was raised.* I Corinthians 6:14.
6. *"all be changed."* I Corinthians 15:51.
7. *spiritual bodies,* I Corinthians 15:46.
8. *"to the ends of the earth."* Acts 1:8.
9. *"with Christ."* I Corinthians 12:12.
10. *"lives in me."* Galatians 2:19-20.
11. *"persecute me?"* Acts 9:4.
12. *welcomes God.* Matthew 10:40.
13. *under his authorization.* Luke 10 ff.
14. *treated him.* Matthew 10:1-25.
15. *"mortal flesh."* 2 Corinthians 4:10-11.
16. *"lives in me."* Galatians 2:20.
17. *on me.* John 6, paraphrased.
18. *to have sex.* Genesis 4:1.
19. *alone in marriage.* Ephesians 5:21 ff.
20. *"of the lamb."* Revelation 19:7.
21. *world might believe.* John 17:22.
22. *"glass, darkly."* I Corinthians 13 KJV.
23. *"not yet see,"* Romans 8:25.
24. *"[wandering] sheep,"* John 10:11.
25. *at the table one evening.* Luke 22:19, paraphrased.
26. *he'll be there.* Matthew 18:20.
27. *"world to himself."* 2 Corinthians 5:19.
28. *of his return.* John 14:3.
29. *to God.* Colossians 1:20.
30. *fully redeemed.* Titus 2:14.
31. *"see God's glory."* Isaiah 66:18.
32. *"be welcomed home."* Isaiah 40:5.
33. *"all in all."* Colossians 3:11.
34. *"come near."* Luke 10:9.
35. *to Jesus' tomb . . .* See Luke 24:4 ff.
36. *"seeing a ghost."* Luke 24:37.
37. *"close of the age."* Matthew 28:20.
38. *"and the Spirit."* John 3:5.
39. *that of Ezekiel.* Ezekiel 37:1-14.
40. *or 2 Maccabees.* 2 Maccabees 7:9, 14.
41. *return to it.* Genesis 3:19.
42. *"some doubted."* Matthew 28:17.
43. *yet to be revealed.* Ephesians 1:14.
44. *"ought to say."* Luke 12:11-12.
45. *in Nazareth,* Luke 4:14 ff.
46. *"by the Holy Spirit."* I Corinthians 12:3.
47. *"have eternal life,"* From end of John's Gospel.
48. *force to rob.* Luke 3:10 ff.
49. *"in the field."* Matthew 21:28-32.
50. *"does my will."* Matthew 7:22.
51. *the Hebrew Scriptures.* Matthew 12:3, 5; 19:4, etc.

CPSIA information can be obtained at www.ICGtesting.com
Printed in the USA
BVOW05s2351260214

346128BV00008B/125/P